The Indian Dispossessed

JOSEPH, NEZ PERCE CHIEF

(1897)

The

Indian Dispossessed

By
Seth K. Humphrey

*With 16 Full-page Illustrations
from Photographs*

"No man has a place or a fair chance
to exist under the Government of the
United States who has not a part in it"

Revised Edition

Boston
Little, Brown, and Company
1906

Published September, 1905

THE UNIVERSITY PRESS, CAMBRIDGE, U. S. A.

PREFACE

IF the introductory chapter of this book be deemed to bear too heavily upon long-cherished American ideals, will the reader generously consider it as no more than a friendly challenge to discover, in the Indian tales which follow, that those ideals have borne, unsullied, the practical test ?

Not once is there question of the high impulses or fair intent of the American people; but a good intention loses virtue with age, and sentiments which persist without developing into action can weigh little against the plain record of facts.

This is no attempt to maintain that "all men are created equal." In the light of all that is best in human history, that declaration attains to nothing more real than a praiseworthy sentiment mistaken for a fact. Whether the nation which gave it birth has developed it into a sentiment to be honored, or into a grotesque absurdity, during its long contact with a race created *not* the white man's equal, the reader is left to determine.

S. K. H.

CONTENTS

ILLUSTRATIONS

Pyramids

The Indian Dispossessed

INTRODUCTION

THOSE of us whose Latin is of the vintage of two or three decades ago may remember Jacobs' Roman History, with its traditional fables of Italy's earliest days, done in easy Latin for beginners; and some may recall the first plunge into Latin translation: "Antiquissimis temporibus Saturnus in Italiam venisse dicitur," — "In most ancient times Saturn is said to have come into Italy." Then the next sentence disclosed, after due persuasion, that he founded a city, and called it Saturnia; and finally, at the close of this first paragraph, the first word of the Italian people: " Hic Italos primus agriculturam docuit," from which, with much thumbing of the " vocabulary " in the back part of the book, we learned that — " He first taught the Italians agriculture." There, in a nutshell, — or, rather, in a sentence, — is the beginning of Italian civilization; and the beginning was in agriculture — the fundamental art, an art so old among the Italians that its origin was ascribed to Deity.

The Indian Dispossessed

Since then, those who hold the magic wand of civilization have come, many times the world over, into the land of the unenlightened, with all shades of motives, and with all sorts of teachings; but the point of it all is that this mythological benefactor began the civilization of his chosen people, not by teaching them the alphabet, nor a new creed, nor to make bead-work for the curio market, but — "*He first taught the Italians agriculture.*"

From Italy's beginning to the first page of the American aborigine's story may seem a far cry. It is. Their significant relation — if a hibernicism be permissible — is that of dissimilarity. Had some kindly Saturn preceded the Pilgrims in the land, and *first taught the Indians agriculture,* the meeting of the races might have resulted very differently; but it was decreed that the Indian should receive his first impression of the better life from mere mortals.

While the good Puritans appear to have yearned for the salvation of the Indian's soul, they labored more effectively for the possession of the Indian's land; and with a quick perception of their prime motive the Indian soon brought himself to see, above all else in the new civilization, a despoiler of his one possession — the great hunting-ground of his fathers. So, under the persuasive influence of these conditions, the Indian moved continually westward, with his heart full of hate for the white man, and the first great lesson in civilization still unlearned.

2

Introduction

Musing, some twenty years ago, upon these prickly points in his country's history, a brilliantly satirical member of the United States Senate disguised the unpalatable truths in a pellet of humor, thus, — "When the pilgrim fathers landed upon the New England shore, they first fell upon their knees, and then upon the aborigines," — and, forthwith, the American people assimilated an unwelcome historical *Resemblance* mess without so much as making a wry face. Indeed, this witticism is now so respectably ancient that it is here repeated with much trepidation, and only because *Trembling* there are so few oases of humor in the grim desert of the Indian's story that the reader may do well to fortify himself here with a smile, against the heat of other emotions during his journey toward the end of the book.

With the coming of the troublous times that led to the Revolution the good fathers found themselves in the rôle of the oppressed, — and then, how changed their views of man's rights! The youthful nation announced to the world the discovery of these mighty Truths in human affairs, — "That all men are created equal; that they are endowed by their Creator with certain inalienable rights, among them being life, liberty and the pursuit of happiness."

In the calm light of this day it passes the understanding that a people burdened with the problem of two inferior races — one, slaves, and the other, not slaves only because they possessed not one attribute of

The Indian Dispossessed

the slave — should have thus expressed themselves with any literal intent. It is a kindness to absolve them from any intent within the real meaning of the pronunciamento, for we see now that it voices a helpful aspiration, not a fact; but what more was it then than an impassioned protest against inequality with those *above*, without one thought of those *below*, — a self-centering cry, " None shall be set above us!" and not the voice of love, saying, " Arise, my brother, and stand with me "?

It is with some hesitation that the pet fiction of the American people is thus vigorously assailed, but while there remains any of the substance with which we have invested its vague indefiniteness the true status of the Indian cannot be clearly defined, and until the limits of his rights are known we cannot know to what extent those limits have been overstepped. If we believe that, in any literal sense, the Indian was created the equal of " all men," and endowed by his Creator with the inalienable right to the pursuit of happiness in his own way, we have sinned — and that enormously, because against our own conception of right — in even disturbing him in the possession of his vast hunting-ground; a view untenable, because we know that in this we have done only that which dominant peoples have done since the beginning, and will continue to do until civilization shirks its duty to develop the resources of the whole earth for the highest good of mankind.

4

Introduction

Then put aside the fallacy, and say, that no Indian is the equal of the white man until he has turned to the white man's way; his possessory right to the great hunting-ground of his fathers conferred upon him no ownership, in the white man's sense of ownership, in land fitted for the higher uses of civilization; no precious metals in the hills were his, because for generations he had chased the buffalo and the deer over the surface.

The untamed Indian had but one tangible right, — the right to be shown the new way by those who had made his own way impossible. The very dearth of his rights as a savage measured the white man's tremendous obligation to bring him, by all reasonable means, into the rights that come with civilization. That the Indian did not turn readily to the better way, history makes us sure; the change demanded was too abrupt, too opposed to his inbred notions of labor and responsibility; but civilization was not to be stayed by the Indian's refusal to accept its teachings, and in just proportion to his unbending the Indian went down before it. This was the *main* tragedy in the Indian's story, and his well-meaning friends have often, in a spirit of undiscriminating sentimentalism, made of it the main indictment against the white man. Of this indictment we may at once acquit ourselves, in so far as we have unselfishly and intelligently labored to make the new way attractive; but to no greater extent, for history again shows clearly that among the most implacable and bitter of all Indians were many who had once turned to the white man, only to be met with treachery and deceit.

The inevitable results of this long, unequal contest were made more tragic because of the unyielding Indian's conviction that his right to " life, liberty and the pursuit of happiness " was being ruthlessly trampled upon. There was no difference, to his untutored mind, between defending his native land against the incursions of other wild tribes, as he had often defended it, and his final contest with the white man. There was the same bitterness in defeat, the falling of his braves was as tragic, and the sufferings of his women and children as real, as though he were yielding to another barbarian, because — Heaven help him — there was much in the white man's philosophy which he could not understand. In the calm of the long afterward, when we sing our song of liberty:

> " I love thy rocks and rills,
> Thy woods and templed hills,"

it will do the Indian no more than a sentimental justice to remember it as the song of his own glad days.

The tragic story of the untamed, fighting Indian is closed, and this book will have no more of him, — thus eliminating many a sad, but possibly instructive, chapter. Neither is the tale to be burdened with a recital of individual atrocities perpetrated by irresponsible white settlers, and by renegades

who so largely constituted the ragged, cutting edge
of our civilization, — a profitless harrowing of the
sensibilities, unless one delights in instances of uncontrolled depravity. It is with the Indian coming
into his rights as a man through the fundamental
art of agriculture, — how his rights in the real ownership of land have been conserved, and how violated,
under regularly constituted authority; and especially
with the acts of that prime arbiter of the Indian's
destiny, the United States Congress, that these narratives have to do.

With the final placing of the Indians upon reservations thirty, forty, and fifty years ago the Government found itself, for the first time in its history, in
full control of the Indian situation — and, consequently, for the first time with full responsibility for
the Indian's care and civilization. The Indian's game
— his livelihood — had disappeared before the advancing white man. He was subdued, generally
friendly, and in a mood as receptive as the Indian
mind is capable of. To turn him from the responsibilities of the tribal life to the first responsibilities of
the civilized life was clearly to turn him from the
pursuit of game for a living to the pursuit of agriculture for a living. That was the way involving the
least abrupt transition; from the buffalo and the deer
to stock-raising, from the gathering of roots and
berries to the gathering of vegetables; and with this,
education and Christian teaching. None but the very

7

sanguine could hope that most, or even a large majority, of the Indians would take readily to the new way, but this was the natural way, the shortest step, and the first step, and the Government set out in good faith to *first teach the Indians agriculture*.

In view of subsequent history it is instructive to read in the agency reports of forty and fifty years ago of the earnestness and industry that characterized the Indian's beginning in agriculture and stock-raising. It does seem as though the very pathos of his simple efforts would have impressed upon the Government with new force the *double* right of the agricultural Indian to the *best* of the land, and protection upon it during his long endeavor to come into the better way, — the right of a man striving to do a man's work, and his prior traditional right to all the land.

But the great, voting public's interest in the Indian has been sentimental, not material, — often at a high pitch over some newly revealed injustice, but always effervescent, and rarely persisting until election day; and Congress — created by votes, perpetuated by votes, recognizing sentiment only as expressed in votes — has always in Indian affairs more or less narrowly represented the interests of the voters on the frontier, uninfluenced by public sentiment.

The typical frontiersman was a survival of strenuous conditions; a man of forceful action, with an insatiable desire for more land, and the *best* land,

Introduction

and land always just over the border laid down in the latest covenant with the Indian, even though covered with the crops of Indians turned to the white man's way. His development of the new country was significant of strength and virility; it extended the bounds of civilization, and, in his rough way, he knew of civilization's debt to him and his kind.

The neighbor of this man was an untutored, subdued child of nature, taking his first lesson in the pioneer's own well-mastered art. He was not a voter, — not even a man, in the eyes of the law. His efforts were those of a beginner, — uncertain, lacking efficiency, and of little economic effect.

How else could such a man as the pioneer regard this primitive school in the wilderness, and these little beginnings, than as a sentimental effort of small consequence in the general scheme? The Indian's right and the white man's obligation were nothing to him. He had seen the less forceful of his own kind go down to failure before the obstacles which he himself had overcome, and he measured the worth of both Indian and white man alike by the test of strength and efficiency. The abandoned efforts of his departed white neighbor had inured to his benefit, and he looked with anticipation upon the Indian's small improvements as the next in order to come. To develop new country was his business, and in his greater ability to develop its resources he thought he saw his better right to the Indian's land.

The Indian Dispossessed

This was the man who was to determine the Indian's right to a foothold in his own country, through congressmen and other officials who *must heed* the demands of their few real electors or be turned out of office. In the game of politics this much of the nation's great trust has been consigned to his gentle hand.

Out of this condition came our great national reproach. Always of his best the Indian gave up to his white neighbor. New treaties curtailing his reservation were entered into, often unwillingly on his part, or old treaties were violated, and each time the Indian moved to portions of his country more remote and less desirable. The lack of permanency made any continued effort in agriculture impossible. With protection in the pursuit of agriculture, the Indian might have learned much; the strenuous game of the "survival of the fittest" in which he found himself taught him nothing better than was in his own philosophy, and too often he turned back to the old way.

Whether he were the defenceless beginner of the Northwest, or the skilful agriculturist of the Southwest desert with ancient systems of irrigation, the Indian was never regarded as a man. The forceful settler dispossessed the irrigating Indian with even less than usual formality because his highly cultivated lands were the more valuable, — either by driving him into the desert and pre-empting his land, or by diverting his water, thus making his land a desert. Typical of these Indians were the four thousand Pimas of

Introduction

' Arizona. They had practised agriculture by irrigation along the Gila River for more than three centuries. In the language of the early records, " They are farmers and live wholly by tilling the soil, and in the earlier days of the American history of the Territory they were the chief support of both the civil and military elements of this section of the country."

In 1886 the whites began to divert the waters of the Gila River. A suit in the federal court was talked of to maintain the clear rights of the Indians, but never pressed. No district attorney who would prosecute such a case against voting white men could expect to live politically. Within seven years the Pimas were reduced from independence to the humiliation of calling for rations, while the white settlers used the Indians' water undisturbed.

" Enough has been written about the need of water for the starving Indians to fill a volume," wrote the discouraged agent, after ten years. " It has been urgently presented to your honorable office time and again, and yet the need of water is just as great and the supply no greater." So the years went on. In 1900 came the cry from the desert, " This water, their one resource, their very life, has been taken from them, and they are, perforce, lapsing into indolence, misery, and vice." Thirty thousand dollars was appropriated for more rations.

Finally, after eighteen years, the suit to recover the Indians' rights received its final quietus. The district attorney reported in 1904: " There is no doubt but that the case could be taken up and prosecuted to a favorable ending, but . . . *it would be impossible for the court to enforce its decree,* and the expense of prosecuting such suit would cost between twenty and thirty thousand dollars."

This Government long ago lost the right to say that it *could not* enforce a federal law against less than a thousand of its agricultural citizens. Its officials *would not* disturb the political balance of Arizona.

Agriculturists one hundred years before the pilgrims landed; agriculturists until white men stole their water; now, looking pitifully for rain in a rainless country. " No rain has fallen for more than a year," says the report of 1904, " consequently they were cut off from any agricultural achievements, but found employment in various ways. The men worked on the railroad, on farms, and in the adjacent towns. The building of the Tonto Reservoir afforded work for many. The women do laundry work, cook, raise chickens, make baskets, and in many ways keep the wolf from the door."

The crime of it cannot be charged to the frontiersman; it is upon the Government that surrendered this portion of its trust to those who were unfit to administer it. It was a trust involving the welfare of a race not contemplated in our free institutions — an unrepresented people under a representative government. The Indian was left without the protection which comes from a sustained public interest, for a sustained public interest is impossible except as it appeals in some measure to public selfishness.

But there is another side to this picture. During all these years of trouble, the Indian was faithfully attended by a great Unselfishness, always striving to re-establish him, to educate and enlighten him. The Government met with no opposition in administering this portion of its trust, and the workers were granted its most generous and intelligent support; for the high ideals of the people have always been the Government's inspiration, even though it be often led to action by a selfish few.

It is not within the scope of this book to recount the great good that has come to the Indian through this branch of the Indian service, save to make full acknowledgment here of its greatness. It has done much more than attend the Indian's education. Many a tribe, and many individual Indians, have had saved to them tracts of *good land,* upon which they have worked their way toward civilization. Indeed, had it not been for the constant presence of these among the Indians who labored for their good, little good land would have been left to any Indians.

These are the two great influences which have shaped the Indian's destiny; one, steadily hewing away the foundation — his land; the other, faithfully moulding the superstructure — his education; both generously supported by a vote-seeking Congress.

The Indian Dispossessed

Where the first has failed, the Indian is coming into full citizenship through agriculture, education, and Christian teaching. Where both have succeeded in their opposing efforts, we find the Indian figuratively, and often literally, on the rocks; educated, saved, and forlorn, — amiable, but aimless, in his arrested development. He has missed the fundamental lesson of mankind.

But, too often, without the foundation of good land the superstructure has fallen, — and upon us is responsibility for the most miserable being in the land; landless, idle, drunken, dirty, and altogether unattractive; for forty years discouraged in agriculture and encouraged in mendicancy under the ration system, — a degenerate by-product of our nation-building process.

Much that was vicious in the administration of Indian affairs has been eliminated during recent years. The system of Indian education was never better, never more liberally supported by the Government, and in allotting good land in severalty to Indians whose reservations still contain good land, we are fulfilling our obligation to those individual Indians. But from the portion of the nation's trust which fell into the political pot we have the barren reservations, perpetuated for many thousands of Indians of the second and third generation whom we must, perforce, continue to support, or " civilize " as railroad section hands, and ditch diggers, and sellers of bead-work, while the white man cultivates their good land. We

14

Introduction

now show a belated eagerness to square ourselves with
these Indians by allotting to them their choice of land
from the poor remnants which have been left to them
after the many choosings of the white man, — a
pathetic spectacle, this granting Indians the *choice* of
land on which no well-equipped white man could make
a living. This portion of our great obligation is
beyond redemption.

When we hear of dark injustice among the natives
of Africa, or in Russia's Siberian wastes, we turn in
horror from the oppressed to vent indignation upon
the oppressor. But when the tale of our own Poor
Lo is told, we lift our eyes to Heaven — not being so
well able to see ourselves as to see others — and mur-
mur, reverently, " 'T is the Survival of the Fittest! "
Those who think lightly are wont to exclaim, impa-
tiently, that the Indian's story is a closed book. It is
— nearly so; but the book of history is never closed,
except by those who think lightly.

Ugly facts never stood out more plainly. In this
Indian business Congress has persistently betrayed
the nation's ideals at the behest of a small fraction of
the people; the Rosebud land scandal of 1904 (told
in the chapter, " Uncle Sam, Trustee ") shows that
it can be led as easily now as ever before. If in our
self-satisfied conceit we think that *other* businesses
have not led, and are not now leading, Congress to
other betrayals of public trust, we, too, may as well
say that history can tell us nothing, and close the book.

The Indian Dispossessed

Congress delivers to the highest political bidder. If the public bids highest, it is because of some great selfish interest. The Indian's welfare, involving the nation's honor, was struck off to the vicious few because, forsooth, it was not spelled in dollars before the public eye.

This states a condition, not a remedy; the remedy lies — in a slumber that knows no waking — with the great public, — a public content that its ideals are so little represented in national legislation.

And now, as we explore the darker recesses of the Indian's story, we need not forget that the light still shines outside; and while we watch the stain of what we did trickling down over the snowy whiteness of our first good intentions, some may find solace in the placid, self-centering philosophy of these nameless lines : —

> " Hapless mosquito ! settling on my head,
> I give one gentle tap, and thou art dead.
> On such a day, to slay e'en thee I 'm loath —
> Would that the world were wide enough for both ! "

THE INDIAN RESERVATION

FIFTY years of the American Indian's story lies in the Indian Reservation. Year by year the story comes first-hand in the reports of each reservation agent to the Commissioner of Indian Affairs; the Honorable Commissioner presents a review of the reports, with his comments and recommendations, to the Secretary of the Interior; and the Honorable Secretary embodies a brief of it in his annual report to the President. Then there are the Indian treaties (so-called, Heaven knows why), a whole bookful of them, with Uncle Sam as party of the first part, and Uncle Sam as absolute custodian of the party of the second part; and Executive Orders, in which the signature of the President makes and unmakes Indian country without the troublesome formality of consulting the Indians. And, too, when the Indian thinks his right to " life, liberty, and the pursuit of happiness " extends beyond the confines of his reservation into his old hunting-grounds, the story shifts to the War Department, and Generals, Colonels, and Majors take a hand at the record.

So the Indian story threads its way through the various public documents, from eighteen hundred and fifty-five to nineteen hundred and five. It is the object of this book to pick out the official narratives of a few Indian tribes and present the Indian in his unromantic reality, — not the Indian in paint and feathers chasing the buffalo, nor the Indian of Cooper, but a forlorn individual wrested from old conditions and brought face to face with new; a being bearing the impress of a common Maker at the absolute mercy of those who profess that "all men are created equal." The public documents shall tell most of the story.

The first forcible exposition of the reservation system, somewhat revised and in working order, appears in the report for 1872 of the Commissioner of Indian Affairs to the Honorable Secretary of the Interior. He says in part:

"In the first announcement made of the reservation system, it was expressly declared that the Indians should be made as comfortable on, and as uncomfortable off, their reservations as it was in the power of the Government to make them; that such of them as went right should be protected and fed, and such as went wrong should be harassed and scourged without intermission. It was not anticipated that the first proclamation of this policy to the tribes concerned would effect the entire cessation of existing evils; but it was believed that persistence in the course marked out would steadily reduce the number of the refractory, both by the

losses sustained in actual conflict and by the deser-
tion of individuals as they should become weary of
a profitless and hopeless struggle, until, in the near
result, the system adopted should apply without exception to all the then roving and hostile tribes.
Such a use of the strong arm of the Government
is not war, but discipline."

Not war — certainly not; but discipline. It is
fairly alive with discipline. If some captious reader
persists in the notion that every war of conquest
since the world began aimed to "steadily reduce the
number of the refractory," both by killing and by
strangling hope in the living, he may content himself with the reflection that, sometimes, discipline
is hell.

So the well-disposed Indian was to revel in
plenty, and the hostile, "scourged without intermission." How did it work?

The Government soon discovered three things: first,
that the well disposed and subjugated tribes could be
kept in a state of quiet at an extremely small expense,
simply because they would not or could not fight;
second, that by providing for the powerful and semi-
hostile tribes so bountifully as to allay their resent-
ment of the intrusion, the white settlements could gain
foothold far up into the Indian country without the
aid of the military; and third, that while the system
of rewards to the righteous was correct as a sentimental proposition, the same amount of money ex-

pended on the Indians in *inverse* ratio to their friendliness produced the best results — for the Government. Hence a curiously "Inverted Policy" in full blast at the time of the Commissioner's report. Here is his apology for it:

"This want of completeness and consistency in the treatment of the Indian tribes by the Government has been made the occasion of much ridicule and partisan abuse; and it is indeed calculated to provoke criticism and to afford scope for satire; but it is none the less compatible with the highest expediency of the situation. It is, of course, hopelessly illogical that the expenditures of the Government should be proportioned not to the good but to the ill desert of the several tribes; that large bodies of Indians should be supported in entire indolence by the bounty of the Government simply because they are audacious and insolent, while well-disposed Indians are only assisted to self-maintenance, since it is known they will not fight."

Although "hopelessly illogical," it was held to be *reasonable:*

"It is not a whit more unreasonable that the Government should do much for hostile Indians and little for friendly Indians than it is that a private citizen should, to save his life, surrender all the contents of his purse to a highwayman; while on another occasion, to a distressed and deserving applicant for charity, he would measure his contribution by his means and disposition at the time. There is precisely the same

The Indian Reservation

justification for the course of the Government in feeding saucy and mischievous Indians to repletion, while permitting more tractable and peaceful tribes to gather a bare subsistence by hard work, or what to an Indian is hard work."

The friendly Indian seems to have been quick to perceive the penalty for being a good Indian, but, unfortunately for his peace of mind, he was unable to read this lucid explanation of the reasonableness of his affliction.

That the Commissioner was strenuous in his views regarding the early reduction of the hostile Indian to the inexpensive variety, may be gathered from the following extracts:

" It belongs not to a sanguine, but to a sober view of the situation, that three years will see the alternative of war eliminated from the Indian question, and the most powerful and hostile bands of to-day thrown in entire helplessness on the mercy of the Government. . . .

" No one certainly will rejoice more heartily than the present Commissioner when the Indians of this country cease to be in a position to dictate, in any form or degree, to the Government; when, in fact, the last hostile tribe becomes reduced to the condition of suppliants for charity. This is, indeed, the only hope of salvation for the aborigines of the continent. If they stand up against the progress of civilization and industry, they must be relentlessly crushed. The westward course of population is neither to be denied nor delayed for the sake of all the Indians that ever called this country their home. They must yield or perish; and there is something that savors of providential mercy in the rapidity with which their fate advances upon them, leaving them scarcely the chance to resist before they shall be surrounded and disarmed. . . .

" The freedom of expansion which is working these results is to us of incalculable value. To the Indian it is of incalculable cost. Every year's advance of our frontier takes in a territory as large as some of the kingdoms of Europe. We are richer by hundreds of millions; the Indian is poorer by a large part of the little that he has. This growth is bringing imperial greatness to the nation; to the Indian it brings wretchedness, destitution, beggary."

So " expansion " and " imperial greatness " are not terms born of the Philippine situation. The business dates back some thirty years.

" Discipline " of the strenuous kind proceeded with the reduction of the hostile Indian in strict accordance with the good old law of " the Survival of the Fittest," despite the handicap of the Slogan. And it is beyond the expectation of reason that a sentimental expression of " inalienable rights," at best the cry of a distressed people even though still persisting as a living truth, should have secured to the Indian as his game preserve vast areas of country fitted for infinitely better uses. Such a thing cannot happen until the laws made " in the beginning " become subject to human revision.

But after that, the host of " suppliants "; and then, what next? Then, surely, there is grand opportunity for the play of the humanitarian professions of a great nation; with the last Indian turning to his " Great Father " for instruction in the better way, will Justice be invited to preside over the destiny of the unhappy race? Or will Uncle Sam " measure his contribution by his means and disposition at the time," and let it go at that?

THE UMATILLAS

" I look at this land, this earth; it is like my mother, as if she was giving me milk, for from it I draw the food on which I live and grow." *The plea of an Oregon Indian Chief.*

" These poor people, relying on the promises of their 'Great Father' for protection, prefer to keep their little homes and die by the graves of their fathers, and nothing remains but to do them simple justice and protect them in their rights." *The Response of One Good Man in Authority.*

FIFTY years ago, the Indians living in the valleys and mountains where Oregon, Washington, and Idaho meet, first heard the white man's cry of Gold. Onward came the excited miners, reckless with gun and regardless of rights, and away sped the Indians' game. The Indians gazed in wrathful consternation. What should they do?

"Fight," said the chiefs. "Fight for the land of our fathers!" echoed the warriors. And fight they did, with the desperate ferocity of men who know that in the end they must lose. And they lost.

Then in 1859 the Government gathered up the remnants of three tribes, — the Walla Wallas, the Cayuse, and the Umatillas, — made a treaty with them, and placed them all together on a reservation in northeastern Oregon.

24

The Umatillas

In consideration for the cession of their vast hunting-grounds, which included the exceedingly valuable Walla Walla valley, this Umatilla reservation was secured to them, with certain annuities and other benefits, including an agency for their protection and instruction in farming, and a school for the education of their children. They then settled down to learn to " travel the white man's road."

Seven years later their agent has this to say about them:

" I estimate the number of acres now under fence at something over two thousand, about half of which is unbroken land used for pasture, hay, corrals, etc., the remainder being in a good state of cultivation. The number of acres planted this year may be estimated as follows: Wheat, 480 acres; corn, 120 acres; oats, 100 acres, with about 200 acres in peas, beans, barley, potatoes, melons, pumpkins, onions, turnips, carrots, parsnips, beets, cabbage, and other vegetables. The approximate yield of this land will be fifteen thousand bushels of all kinds of produce, more than sufficient for the wants of all if equally distributed.

" As usual, quite a number of Indian farmers will each have from five hundred to one thousand dollars' worth of produce to sell, which they can dispose of for good prices at the neighboring towns and stations on the road. . . .

" Most of the Indians residing here are Roman

Catholics, and their attachment to the reverend
father, who is pleased to act as their spiritual as
well as temporal teacher, is very great. . . .

" The only violations of law and order are committed by thoughtless young men and renegades from
distant reservations."

And the State Superintendent adds: " At the annual fair of the Oregon State Agricultural Society,
held in 1865, two first premiums and one second
premium were awarded to these Indians for agricultural products; and I may add that I know, from
personal observation, that products of similar or
even superior quality are by no means uncommon
among them."

A truly pastoral community. Their number is
given as seven hundred and fifty-nine, and thirty-
one scholars are enrolled in the school. Eighty-five
hundred of their horses and cattle graze upon the
reservation.

But the Superintendent's report to the Commissioner of Indian Affairs indicates that the white
men are beginning to repent of their " treaty " with
these Indians:

" The superior quality of the land, and its location on a great thoroughfare, convenient to the gold-
mines of Powder River, Boisé Basin, Oughee, and
other points, of course make it attractive to whites.
There are constant attempts to encroach upon it,
constant attempts, under various pretexts, to locate

SEMEO, — UMATILLA

(1871)

upon it, and occasional attempts to exasperate the Indians into the commission of some overt act which will justify, or at least palliate, retaliation, and thus give an excuse for plunging the country into another Indian war, the end of which, they well know, would be the expulsion of the Indians from the coveted tract."

And their agent confirms the presence of the cloud that hangs over these children of the forest:

" The only cause of discontent existing in their minds is the constant fear that the reservation will be taken from them and thrown open to settlement by the whites."

Again, in the following year: " The Indians, who are superior to most tribes in intellect and energy, are very much attached to their home, and very reluctant to abandon it. Some thoughtless whites have talked quite freely about driving the Indians off and taking possession by force. During a visit last spring to that agency and vicinity I heard threats of that sort repeated many times. Public meetings of citizens have been held to devise means to have the tract opened for settlement, and petitions for the same object to Congress and to the State Legislature have been circulated and numerously signed. The Indians are hence very uneasy and very much alarmed. There are here, as on probably every frontier, a few reckless villains who desire to provoke a war."

The Indian Dispossessed

Two years later comes this plain, blunt communication from their agent:

" I believe it is as well known by you, as it is by everybody in the country, that this place is wrongly situated for an Indian reservation. It is closely surrounded by white settlements, and contains nearly all the good land in Umatilla County; in fact, there is a larger area of cultivatable land in one body on the reserve than anywhere else in eastern Oregon."

" Wrongly situated " because it is too good for these farmer Indians. But why too good? After stating that the whites have already opened several roads through the reservation, he concludes:

" With this situation of affairs it is not surprising that the whole white population of this region are clamorous for the removal of the Indians from this tract of land, which would soon be developed into a rich and populous country."

Assuming that the agricultural Indian is at least entitled to an advantageous foothold in the land of his fathers, it is interesting to note the effect of these various messages in Washington.

The tales of attempts to encroach upon and exasperate the Indians, of the threats and consequent terror of the Indians at the thought of being driven from their homes, seem to have spent themselves upon the desert air. But now, " the whole white population of this region are clamorous for the removal of the Indians," and things begin to move. Within two months of this "clamorous" report, the Commissioner of Indian Affairs, in his report to the Secretary of the Interior, re-states the case in more diplomatic form:

" The question has been raised whether they should not be removed to some other locality, as they are constantly annoyed by the encroachments of the whites, who covet the possession of their fertile and valuable lands, lying, as they do, on the highway to Boisé City and Salt Lake. The Superintendent recommends the appointment of a commission to arrange for a sale of their lands, and their settlement upon some other reservation."

This is plain enough. The Indians must not be annoyed. They may have to give up their homes to the covetous whites and move to the wilderness, but *they must not be annoyed.*

The plan to remove the Indians developed rapidly. Congress soon resolved:

" That the President of the United States is hereby requested to negotiate with Indians upon the Umatilla reservation, in Oregon, with the view of ascertaining on what terms said Indians will relinquish to the United States all their claims or rights to said reservation and remove to some other reservation in said State or Washington Territory."

A commission of three was duly appointed, consisting of the State Superintendent, who had recommended their removal, the resident agent of the

The Indian Dispossessed

Indians, and a farmer, a former Indian trader, whose land adjoined the reservation. The summer of 1871 finds the special commissioners on the reservation, ready for business.

And the Indians! All is excitement and consternation. The crisis is upon them; the men from the Great Father have come to make another bargain! Come forth, chiefs; make the plea of your lives in defence of the Indian country! Make your words strong, but with a good heart, for the Great Father must not be displeased with what the Indians say. Speak from your hearts for this piece of ground, for the words of the white man are many, and the words of the Indian few!

The commissioners came, and the Indians gathered at the agency from all parts of the reservation. Times without number before, commissioners have come, and as many times Indians have gathered to meet them, — shrewd and forceful men, with purpose determined, to bargain with those who know little else than love of native land. Little wonder that the Indian moves each time to a less coveted country, and wonders why the Great Spirit of his fathers has forsaken him.

But in this particular instance the expectant whites reckoned without one man; it is necessary to go back a little. A salient feature of President Grant's " peace policy " was the Board of Indian Commissioners, authorized by special act of Congress, " to

The Umatillas

consist of not more than ten persons, selected from among men eminent for their intelligence and philanthropy, to serve without pecuniary compensation." This Board was the result of an earnest attempt on the part of President Grant to rescue the Indian service from the political mountebanks who trafficked in the welfare of a helpless race to gain the political support of the frontier country. To check the wholesale robbing of Indian supplies, the Board was clothed with authority to approve and supervise all Indian contracts; more especially, the members of the Board were to acquaint themselves with the needs of the Indians by personal visits to the reservations, that they might in some measure stand between the wolfish rapacity of the frontiersmen and the defenceless reservation Indians.

Felix R. Brunot and Vincent Colyer were appointed chairman and secretary, respectively, of the first Board. It is enough to say that they were qualified literally for their distinguished offices — "men eminent for their intelligence and philanthropy." The story of the labors of these men, of their visits to the agencies and Indian camps throughout the great West, of hardships endured for humanity's sake, securing justice, and denying to no lowly Indian the right to be heard in his own behalf, covers the brightest page in Indian history.

Felix R. Brunot appeared with his secretary at

this Council on the Umatilla reservation. Now, the records are full of such councils with reservation Indians; some of them drag along for a month, three months, or all summer, before the desired "consent" is gained. In others, the Commissioners wear themselves out before the Indians give up, and depart, always to come again, prepared to win.

This Council lasted six days — just long enough to carefully present the question of removal to the Indians, and to hear the replies of their chiefs. Possibly it would have lasted no longer had Mr. Brunot not be there. Who knows? But it stands significant among all the land-winning efforts of the white man as the shortest *unsuccessful* council on record.

The surrounding whites were out in force, highly interested spectators; a United States senator for Oregon made one speech to the Indians, in which, amid protestations of friendship, he pictured the overwhelming advance of the white man in a way that must have terrified these simple-minded people.

" . . . The whites will, perhaps, in the course of time, want to build railroads through your reservations, when the President thinks it necessary. The railroads will bring more white people into the country. They may settle about the reservation, and we may not be able to prevent their committing some wrong. If they should commit wrong on the Indians, we fear you would commit some wrong

against them in retaliation. Then the white people
and the Indians might have a great war. There
are great numbers of white people, and we fear they
would exterminate the Indian. This we wish to
prevent. Our hearts are with the Indians, and, as
law-makers, we wish to protect them. We want
them to understand fully the danger that surrounds
them. The President will do all he can to protect them, but there are some bad white men as well
as bad Indians. We want you to think of it, and
decide whether it would be better to get away from
the roads and the railroads that may some time be
built through the country. . . ."

The Indians took little part in the speech-making
of the first two days. The superintendent presented
the question of removal with great elaboration, and
Mr. Brunot gave the Indians several talks of an
advisory nature. Everything said was carefully in-
terpreted and recorded. One Indian — Uma-pine, a
Cayuse chief — interjected remarks at frequent in-
tervals; he seemed suspicious of the superintendent:

" My heart is this way; you thought over it; you
wished for this reservation; you wished for Grand
Ronde, for Walla Walla Valley and Umatilla; you
wished for it. What kind of a heart was it that
wished for all these places? Speak plain and all will
hear it."

But old Uma-pine followed one of Mr. Brunot's
talks with this rather good-humored acknowledgment:

The Indian Dispossessed

" You brought the mind of the Great Father from Washington. I am poor, and I speak; I know nothing; you are a long way ahead of us. You say we are far behind you; that is all right, and we do not mind if you tell us so."

On the third day, after the senator had presented the question of removal in his peculiarly forceful way, the Indian speeches began. Howlish-Wampo, the head chief of the Cayuse, led the defence: [1]

" I heard what you said about our lands, and I understood what you said. We like this country and don't want to dispose of our reservation. I look at this land, this earth; it is like my mother, as if she was giving me milk, for from it I draw the food on which I live and grow. I see this little piece of land; it is all I have left; I know it is good land. This reservation was marked out for me. The people that are on this reservation are working, are doing their own work for themselves. I understand that you are asking me for my land. I say I like my land, and I don't know whether you will fulfil your promise if I accept your promises for my land. I did not see, with my own eyes, the money that was promised me before. All the stock I have had to feed on this land here. That is why I say this little piece of land, all I have here, I want

---

[1] The frequent allusions in the Indians' speeches to Stevens and Palmer, the Council at Walla Walla, and unfulfilled promises, all refer to their treaty.

34

left for me. The large country I gave Governor Stevens, and you have not paid for it. The white man has settled on it. I feel that I have here a small piece of land left, this that I live on now. The whites have all the land outside, and the other reservations are all full of people who belong on them. The Nez Perce are living on their reservation, and the Indians at Simcoe are on their reservation. The Indians below live on Warm Spring reservation. I see that they are all living on their own reservations, and feel just as I do living on mine. The same I said before I say again, I cannot let my reservation go. That is what I have to say now to your commissioners."

Then Wenap-Snoot followed; and Hom-li. Tenale-Temane made a characteristic Indian speech:

"I have heard what you said to me. There is my friend Mr. Brunot; he has just come here; I heard him with my ears and with my heart, and what I heard him say he talked straight. When he talked of God, of Him who made the ground on which we stand, my heart was glad, and I thought he talked straight; this is why I thought we were going to have a straight talk. The whites talked to me some time ago, and I came over here. The land was marked out for me and I came upon it. We have been here eleven years; and since I saw this reservation, I have been on it ever since. I looked and saw with my eyes, there is so much land they have marked out for me. Now, my friend, when I came here, I saw the white man's fences and how they were made, and I went to work. Ever since that I have worked hard. I am an old man; I have worked till the sweat rolled off me to get food for my children; that is the reason for what I have to say now. . . . I do not wish you, my friend, to have bad feelings at what I have said. The President, when he sees what is written, will see what his children have said, and then he will think in his heart that his children (the Indians) love their country. My friend, I tell you again, I love my country; I want to raise my children, and also raise provisions for them on it. That is why I don't want any white man to come and live inside the reservation. That is what Governor Palmer and Governor Stevens told us, that no white man shall go and live inside our reservation. Now, my friend, you have heard what I have said about my land, and that is why I want to stay here; I cannot find any other country outside; my friend, the white man, has occupied the whole country. I see the whites travelling through the country on all sides, but I stay here on these lands that they promised me I should keep."

The Superintendent responded with another long talk about the places to which the Indians might go. He talked so long that Hom-li ended his speech the next day with the remark: " You make speeches too long. All day yesterday you talked. We cannot remember what you say."

Wenap-Snoot replied to the numerous suggestions with one of the shortest and pithiest Indian speeches on record:

" I want to say a few words to answer what you have said. I saw Lapwai (Nez Perce) with my own eyes, and I have seen the mouths of the Yakama with my own eyes; I have seen the Yakama reservation (Simcoe) with my own eyes, and I have seen Walloa Valley with my own eyes, and all the Snake country away South I have seen with my own eyes, and all these countries. I have seen all them with my own eyes, and none of these countries would suit me."

The numerous speeches bring out many interesting phases of Indian thought. The dignified earnestness of all their utterances indicates the seriousness with which the Indians regarded this coming again of the white man. " God hears me now," said Pierre, " and he hears you; we have spoken plainly to one another, and not with bad hearts. I have no wish to go and see that country you talked to us about. I have no wish for any other country."

And Uma-pine: " I believe you think your bodies are dear to you in the same way we value our land. It is dear to us — dear to every one of us. We know every day there is some bargain made."

On the morning of the sixth day some one brought

The Indian Dispossessed

De-co-tisse bad news from home, and, despite his expressed desire to avoid publicity, his sorrowfully humorous tale became a part of the record:

"I don't want what I say written down; I only want to tell you I have been here at the council so many days. You told us you were going to make this matter about the land all plain to us. I left fifty-seven bundles of oats, sixty rows of corn and pumpkins, and all I had, I left them on the ground to attend this council. They are all destroyed. Two cows with bells on, followed by a band of mixed cattle, with mixed brands on them, came in and destroyed them. I do not tell you this from a bad heart; I only wanted to tell you what has happened."

Poor De-co-tisse! Many a patriot has left the plough at his country's call, but few have had their sacrifices heralded with such particularity.

Finally the Indians were told to counsel among themselves and prepare their final answer. There could not have been much doubt about this final answer; as the commissioners withdrew, a Cayuse chief called after them, "You need not wait long; come when you get your dinner!"

And this was the answer:

"HOWLISH-WAMPO. You are asking us now as if you were speaking to our hearts. What you have spoken this people have heard. . . . This reservation that we are on, we all hold it with our bodies and with our souls; and right out here are my father and mother, brothers and sisters and children all buried; and I am guarding their graves. That is my heart, my friend. This reservation, this small piece of land, we look upon it as our mother, as if she were raising us. You come here to ask me for my land. It is like as if we who are Indians were to be sent away and get lost. I look upon all sides. On the outside of the reservation I see your houses. They are good. They have windows in them. You are bringing up your children well; that is why I say this. You must listen to me. I do not want to part with my land. I want to show you white chiefs that that is what my heart is. I do not want you to make my land smaller. If you do, what would my stock feed upon? What is the reason you white men, who live near the reservation, like my land and want to get it? You must not think so. You are not going to get it. I am telling you this as a friend. I am not telling it with a bad heart. I want to know, if I was to go away from here, where I could find as good a piece of land as large as this is? My friends, I tell you now, I wish you would not talk too strong about getting my land. I like my land; will not let it go. That is what makes me talk so. I am showing you my heart about this reservation. You have been asking me for my heart. This is my heart."

" WAT-CHE-TE-MANE. . . . I want you to listen to what I have to say. Here is the way my

heart is. Here in this land my father and mother
and children have died. The father (priest) is the
only one who straightens out my heart. That is
why my heart is this way. I am getting old now,
and I want to die where my father and mother and
children have died. That is why I do not wish to
leave this land and go off to some other land. I
see the church there. I am glad to see it, and think
I will stay beside it and die by the teaching of the
Father. I see how I have sweat and worked in trying to get food. I see the flour-mill the Government
has promised. I have gotten it. I see my friends.
I like all that I have (the mills and lands). That
is why I cannot go away from here. The President
will see the record, and see what we poor old men
have said in this council. What the whites have
tried to show me I have tried to learn. It is not
much, but I have fenced in a small piece of land
and tried to raise grain on it. I am showing you
my heart. I like my church, my mills, my farm,
the graves of my parents and children, and I do not
wish to leave my land. That is all my heart, and
I show it to you."

"PIERRE. I am going to make a short speech.
I have only one heart, only one tongue. Although
you say, ' Go to another country,' my heart is not
that way. I do not wish for any money for my
land. I am here, and here is where I am going to
be. I think all these young men's hearts are like

WOLF, —UMATILLA

(1875)

mine. I think a great deal and have but little to say. What I have said will go on paper to Washington. Then they will think over what we Indians have said. That is all I have to say. I will not part with my lands. And if you should come again I will say the same again. I will not part with my lands."

There was no mistaking the Indian decision; and the Indian decision, according to the view of Mr. Brunot, was what the commissioners came for. That ended the business.

Mr. Brunot concluded the council with words of encouragement and assurance which must have touched the hearts of these harassed Indians. Then he turned to the whites, who had gathered to learn the result of the council, and sent this parting shot:

" I know that there are many persons within reach of this reservation, and other reservations, who suppose that the Indians will be removed, and they are waiting for places on them. These men will be told by their candidates for Congress that they will get the Indians removed. If they should ever succeed, and I do not believe they ever will, it will be with the certainty that the Indians will get the full value of their lands, and I believe the man who waits here to get a pre-emption claim on this land will die a poor man, still waiting. Now, my friends, I never expect to see you again (unless we may hope, as I hope, to meet you in a better world hereafter), and in parting I will venture one word of advice. If I lived near this reservation with the idea of ever living on it I would abandon it at once. I would hitch up my team Monday and I would go to where the Pacific railroad will probably come, or I would settle on some other good place."

Mr. Brunot's report to Washington does not seem to allow the Government much choice of action:

"In view of the maladministration of agents and the misapplication of funds, the failure of the Government to perform the promises of the treaty, and the fact that the Indians have been constantly agitated by assertions that the Government intended their removal, and that their removal was urged for several years in succession in the reports of a former agent (thus taking away from them all incentives to improve their lands), it must be admitted that the progress these Indians have made in ten years has been wonderful. Had they, as the result of the late negotiations, given their consent to removal, I should have felt bound to remonstrate earnestly against any action of the Government to take advantage of so injudicious a decision of their incompetent wards. Happily, the unanimous refusal of the Indians to sell or remove from the remnant of land which the United States has solemnly guaranteed to them, leaves no room for any question of that kind. The arguments used in favor of their removal will apply with equal force to any other

The Umatillas

place to which they might be sent; and even if they did not, these poor people, relying on the promises of their 'Great Father' for protection, prefer to keep their little homes and die by the graves of their fathers, and nothing remains but to do them simple justice and protect them in their rights. It is earnestly hoped that the determination to do so will be authoritatively announced."

But the noble Elect — the gentle frontiersmen who gazed with longing eyes upon the Indian lands — denounced in language picturesque the whole business as an outrageous miscarriage.

And so it was; a miscarriage of injustice.

THE STORY OF THE BITTER ROOT

"If it [the Bitter Root Valley] shall prove, in the judgment of the President, to be better adapted to the wants of the Flathead tribe, . . . then such portions of it as may be necessary shall be set apart as a separate reservation for said tribe." *The National Pledge to the Flatheads.*

SITUATED in the mountainous country at the extreme western edge of Montana is the fertile valley of the Bitter Root, the ancient home of the Flathead Indians. The earliest noteworthy incident in their history dates back to about 1835; the story is rather fancifully told by a Government agent, in a report made many years later:

"Nearly forty years since some Iroquois from Canada, trading with the Flatheads, told them of the teachings of the Jesuit fathers, who for many previous years had been laboring among them, both for their spiritual and temporal good. The Flatheads, listening to these narratives of wonder and love, and as if directed by inspiration from above, selected some of their best men, rude and savage warriors, to proceed to St. Louis and ask a mission to teach them 'the ways of the cross.' Wending their way through the then almost trackless wilds between here and St. Louis, the delegation found

44

The Story of the Bitter Root

itself among a hostile band of Sioux, on the western borders of Missouri, only to be murdered, but one escaping to tell the fate of the rest. In the following year, another and a larger delegation was despatched on this Heaven-inspired duty, which succeeded in reaching the object of their destination, and prevailing on Father De Smet to accompany them to their wild mountain homes — the Flatheads thus becoming the first spiritual children among the red men of that venerated and distinguished Catholic missionary. Located among them, the Pend d'Oreilles soon sought his teachings, and bending their necks to the Christian yoke, both tribes in aggregate were duly received into the church, and to this day, although subject to failings and shortcomings, like the rest of humanity, they (particularly the Flatheads) will compare favorably, at least in morality, with a like number of people anywhere."

The capacity of the Indian nature to absorb and literally follow the teachings of a higher faith was never better illustrated than in the case of these tribes. During the years of warfare that followed the advent of the whites in search of gold, nearly all the tribes in the mountains of the great Northwest, alarmed at the flight of their game — their livelihood — before the reckless white explorers, resisted with the ferocity of despair this invasion of what they regarded as their own country. Throughout these bloody years the Flatheads, the Pend

The Indian Dispossessed

d'Oreilles, and the Nez Perces, three neighboring tribes under Christian teachers, remained steadfast friends of the whites, and under the guidance of their self-sacrificing instructors these Indians supplemented the pursuit of game with increasingly successful attempts at agriculture and stock-raising. But the restless white explorers gradually crowded into the attractive valley of the Bitter Root. Then comes the story of another bargain for the Indian country. In 1855 the Flatheads, numbering something less than five hundred, under the leadership of their old Chief Victor, met in council with commissioners appointed to treat with them for the cession of territory and settlement on a reservation. Some miles to the northward of the Bitter Root, in what was known as the Jocko Valley, there had been set apart a large reservation for the Flatheads, the Pend d'Oreilles, and the Kootenais, and thither it was proposed to remove them. The Pend d'Oreilles and Kootenais were successfully disposed of, but Victor and his people strenuously opposed this measure. They were ready to give up the large territory demanded of them, except their Bitter Root Valley; this they would not cede and remove to a country that did not compare in fertility with their own. Besides, why should they? In that valley they had set up their church, their houses, their farms; it belonged to them; there they had established themselves to learn the ways of the

46

white man, and there they proposed to remain. All argument and persuasion failed to shake their determination; Victor and his men flatly refused to sign a treaty which involved the cession of the beloved land of their fathers.

Now, large interests were dependent upon the signing of this treaty; no Brunot was in attendance to cut off the persuasive tactics of the commissioners. The Bitter Root Valley was only a portion of the coveted territory to be ceded. The treaty *must* be signed.

The white man is resourceful, while the Indian is simple; these two characteristics appear prominently in every treaty council with the Indians. After all other expedients had failed, this clause was added to the document for the special benefit of the Flatheads:

" Article XI. It is, moreover, provided that the Bitter Root Valley, above the Lo-Lo Fork, shall be carefully surveyed and examined, and if it shall prove, in the judgment of the President, to be better adapted to the wants of the Flathead tribe than the general reservation provided for in this treaty, then such portions of it as may be necessary shall be set apart as a separate reservation for said tribe. No portion of the Bitter Root Valley, above the Lo-Lo Fork, shall be opened to settlement until such examination is had and the decision of the President made known."

The Indian Dispossessed

" *If it shall prove, in the judgment of the Presi-dent, to be better adapted to the wants of the Flat-head tribe* — ". " The pledge of the Great Father," the Indians argued; *of course* the land of their fathers was better adapted to their wants than the barren Jocko. With an abiding faith in the nation that gave to them their first instructors in the better way, Victor and his chiefs signed the treaty.

There seems to have followed a subsidence of the wave of immigration to that section of country, and no urgent demand for the evacuation of the valley is in evidence for a considerable period. Victor died a few years later, and the chieftainship of the tribe fell to his son Charlos (sometimes written Charlot), a man full worthy to watch over the affairs of this peaceful community. For seventeen years after the signing of the treaty these Indians were left in un-disturbed possession of their lands, except for the gradual encroachment of the white settlers, and during those years they made most remarkable progress in civilization.

In 1872 their number is given as four hundred and sixty; they have four hundred and fifty acres in cultivation, and fifty-five log-houses furnish them with comfortable homes. Two thousand horses and cattle, and large quantities of grain and vegetables, indicate the thrift of these Indian farmers.

It would seem that if ever a band of Indians struggling toward the light of a higher civilization

were entitled to the earnest consideration of a powerful republic, the Flatheads should have had that recognition; but the surrounding whites were already
clamoring for the Indian possessions.

During all these seventeen years the Bitter Root
Valley had not been "surveyed and examined," nor
had the "judgment of the President" been obtained,
as provided for in the eleventh article of their treaty.
The Indians had not given the question of title another thought. Since Victor signed the treaty, every
succeeding year had made the valley "better adapted
to the wants of the Flathead tribe" than the Jocko or
any other reservation, and the Indians held the national pledge that on this one condition the land was
to be set apart for them as a separate reservation.

Still, the title had never been formally settled in
the Indians; and the whites coveted the valley.
Political wires were manipulated, and Washington
was appealed to; the great Juggernaut which was
to crush this band of Indians began to move.

To dispossess the Flatheads, their title must first
be invalidated under color of law. This necessary
formality required "the judgment of the President."
Here it is, signed by U. S. Grant, President of the
United States:

"EXECUTIVE MANSION, November 14, 1871.

"The Bitter Root Valley, above the Lo-Lo Fork,
in the Territory of Montana, having been carefully

4   49

The Indian Dispossessed

surveyed and examined in accordance with the eleventh article of the treaty of July 16, 1855, concluded at Hell Gate, in the Bitter Root Valley, between the United States and the Flathead, Kootenai, and Upper Pend d'Oreilles Indians, which was ratified by the Senate March 8, 1859, has proved, *in the judgment of the President, not to be better adapted to the wants of the Flathead tribe* than the general reservation provided for in said treaty; it is therefore deemed unnecessary to set apart any portion of said Bitter Root Valley as a separate reservation for Indians referred to in said treaty. It is therefore ordered and directed that all Indians residing in said Bitter Root Valley be removed as soon as practicable to the reservation provided for in the second article of said treaty. . . ."

This effectually cleared the land of the Indian title. One would infer that the general reservation must have been a better land than the Flathead home, although the best portions of the Jocko had long since been taken by the tribes already there. The missionary to the Flatheads wrote an earnest letter of protest, and this is his opinion of the land:

"I am satisfied to say — and I know the ground, every inch — that in that whole flat not a couple of hundred acres of middling farming-land can be taken. Besides, what there is of good land is in small, narrow strips, spots, and patches, far apart one from the other. Hence the necessity of fenc-

50

ing in large tracts of bad land, in order to enclose two or three acres of good soil. The few acres of good farming-land along and on both sides of Finley Creek have been taken up long since by half-breeds, and two or three white men married to Indian women. . . ."

Yet the Bitter Root Valley, with its four hundred and fifty acres of growing crops, its houses and cattle, its Indian church and its Indian graves of many generations, was declared "in the judgment of the President, *not* to be better adapted to the wants of the Flathead tribe" than this unsubdued waste in the Jocko!

President Grant's record as a steadfast friend of the Indian is too secure to be called into question, but this executive order is eloquent of a *system* which can procure the signature of an illustrious president to as black a lie as ever Russia's bureaucracy compelled from the hand of the Czar. Can this business be charged to the American people? Certainly not. Public opinion, whenever it has been sufficiently aroused to take notice of Indian affairs, has invariably been with the Indians. But it can be charged to the extremely *popular* system of government which holds every national official with his ear to the ground, listening to popular clamor. Rule by "the voice of the people" is well enough when *all* the people are interested, but a disinterested, contented people will not take the trouble to rule anything; this relegates local matters, such as the seizing of Indian lands, to the control of a very few — the interested few. Wherever a few faithful voters are gathered together, they can, if they present their demands vociferously, impress their own particular congressman into their service. They become, for him, "the voice of the people"; silent ones do not count. He is the servant, not of the whole American people, but of his immediate constituents. It becomes his business to secure the necessary legislation; no matter how questionable the business may be nor how much opposed to the righteous sentiment of the *whole* people, a congressman cannot rise above the average moral standard of his own clamorous electors if he would hold his political ground. But this imposes no moral strain upon the congressman, unless he be an accident in office. He makes representations to the Indian bureau, backed by documents galore from the anxious settlers, and the case travels from official to official as the expressed " will of the people." He approaches a few other congressmen, each burdened with the wants of his electors; "you support my Indian bill, I vote for your scheme;" the rest will vote "aye" anyway, little knowing whether it is to be a cheese factory for New York City or a junket to Hoboken.

Thus a bit of depravity threads its way, unrecognized, upward through the official line to the Chief Executive. Thus a "vociferous few" obtain national

The Story of the Bitter Root

legislation which would not for a moment bear the scrutiny of the whole people.

The plans for this removal were well laid. The Honorable Commissioner of Indian Affairs, in his report, alluded to these Indians as " the Flatheads and other Indians remaining by sufferance in the Bitter Root Valley," and in the spring Congress passed an act ordering their removal to the Jocko reservation. Within ten weeks of the passage of the removal act special commissioner James A. Garfield (afterward President of the United States) appeared among the Flathead Indians, to acquaint them with the demands of the Government and to secure their removal.

The argument with which they met the mandate of the Government is given in General Garfield's own words:

" Responses were made by the three chiefs, and by several head-men of the tribe, and all of the same tenor. The substance of their views may be thus briefly stated:

" It seemed to be their understanding that they had never given up the Bitter Root Valley, and they were very strongly opposed to leaving it. They insisted, and in this I believe they are partly borne out by the facts, that when the treaty of 1855 was nearly completed, Victor, the Flathead chief, refused to sign it unless he and his people could be permitted to remain in the Bitter Root Valley.

The Indian Dispossessed

" It will be remembered that by that treaty a very large territory was ceded to the United States — a tract extending from near the forty-second parallel to the British line, and with an average breadth of nearly two degrees of longitude; that this territory had long been held in undisputed possession of the Flathead nation, and that, on yielding it, Victor insisted upon holding the Bitter Root, above the Lo-Lo Fork, as a special reservation for the Flatheads proper.

" The chiefs admitted that, under the provisions of the eleventh article, it was left in the power of the President to determine whether the Bitter Root Valley, above the Lo-Lo Fork, should be reserved as the permanent home of the Flatheads. But they insisted that by that article the President was required to have the Bitter Root Valley carefully surveyed and examined, and, if it should be better adapted to the wants of the Flatheads, then it should be made a permanent reservation.

" They insisted that such a survey and examination should have been made immediately after the ratification of the treaty, but that it had never been done at all. That for seventeen years no steps had been taken in regard to it, and they considered the silence of the Government on this subject an admission that the valley was to be their permanent home.

" They further called attention to the fact that they had learned something of civilization, and had

54

done a good deal in the way of cultivating the lands and making the valley a more desirable home. They complained that the schoolmasters, blacksmiths, carpenters, and farmers promised them in the treaty of 1855 had never been sent into the Bitter Root Valley; and all the speakers concluded by the declaration that they claimed the Bitter Root Valley as their home and were wholly unwilling to leave it. They, however, affirmed their steady friendship for the whites and disclaimed any hostile intentions, declaring themselves willing to suffer, peaceably, whatever the Government should put upon them, but that they would not go to the reservation."

But as an officer of the Government commissioned to execute a law already enacted, General Garfield was not in a position to discuss with the Indians the ethics of the situation. It became necessary to inform them that the question was, not whether the order was just or unjust, but, to quote his words, "whether they had decided to disobey the order of the President and the act of Congress." Moreover, he realized, as these Indians could not, the utter futility of an appeal from the decision of the Department; a fertile valley certainly would not be cleared of white men in order that the provisions of an Indian treaty might be fulfilled. And he foresaw, as they could not, the pathetic hopelessness of a long-continued struggle to maintain their homes in this valley if they resisted the command to move.

The Indian Dispossessed

It was explained to the Indians that, by act of Congress, the first fifty thousand dollars received from the sale of their lands were to be used to establish them on the Jocko; but they contended (and General Garfield records his full agreement with them) that the sum was wholly inadequate remuneration, even if they were disposed to relinquish their homes for *any* consideration. They were offered the privilege of taking land in severalty in the Bitter Root if they would break up tribal relations, but the proposition to accept a small tract each out of the large valley which they regarded as their own in its entirety did not appeal to their sense of justice.

Charlos and his people steadfastly refused to go to the reservation, and the council ended with the secession of two sub-chiefs, who, with their following of twenty families, consisting of eighty-one people, consented to remove to the Jocko. General Garfield contented himself with the reflection that when Charlos saw these people comfortably housed and specially favored he would surely follow.

Unfortunately for the Indians, the missionary in charge of the Agency Mission was in Helena at the time of the council. On his return he at once forwarded by letter an appeal for the Indians. He objected strenuously to the location on the Jocko selected for them, and asserted that the land " is mostly rocky and gravellous, and altogether unfit for any agricultural purposes." He continues:

The Story of the Bitter Root

" . . . Such being the case, the consequences can be easily foreseen. Either the Flatheads will not move to that new place, or they will soon abandon it, or if they should remain there the Government will have to feed and support them, since they could never become self-sustaining on it. The first remark I heard from the Indians on this subject, on my return from Helena, was simply this: ' The Great Chief has no heart for the Indians, since he intends to make them settle down on rocks.' . . .

" Besides the two objections above, there is a third one, deserving even more particular consideration. All the Flatheads are practical Catholics. There in the Bitter Root Valley they have a Catholic mission and church to themselves; two of our missionaries live among them to instruct them in their religious duties and minister to them in all their spiritual wants. . . .

" We would have no means to start a new mission for them in their new home. Consequently, those poor Flatheads will be made also necessarily to suffer in what is most dear to them, in what they value more than anything else in this world, viz., their religion and the practice of it. When the whole Flathead tribe will be notified of this fact I doubt not that their unwillingness and repugnance to move thither will be intensely increased.

" Hoping, dear sir, that you will give these my observations the consideration your kindness may deem them to deserve, I beg to remain, respectfully, yours,

"F. L. PALLADINI, S.J.

"In charge of Saint Ignatius Mission.

"HON. JAMES A. GARFIELD, M.C."

This letter was laid before the Secretary of the Interior by General Garfield, but it availed nothing. The good priest had a distorted idea as to what observations were likely to impress the Indian bureau.

Then began a record unparalleled in Indian history for unique features. Charlos and his four hundred, clinging with Indian faith to the promise in the eleventh article of their treaty, determined to stand by their homes and passively await the action of their Great Father in Washington; "to suffer, peaceably, whatever the Government should put upon them," as they had said to General Garfield.

The Indian ring was in a quandary. To grant the demands of the "Vociferous Few," call out the military, and remove the inoffensive Indians by force would advertise the malodorous record to the country, with the certainty that swift condemnation of the whole business would follow. On the other hand, to redeem the national pledge required the removal of the whites from the Indians' land, besides congressional and executive acts in *reverse* order — a retreat unprecedented, impossible.

The Story of the Bitter Root

Finally a plan of peaceful reduction was developed. All the benefits and protection provided for in their treaty were withdrawn, and the Flatheads were left to shift for themselves, — a little, independent people closely encircled by a hungry horde of frontiersmen. Their history from this time appears year by year in the reports of the Jocko agent.

One year; the agent writes:

" I have visited most of the Indian lodges and houses in the Bitter Root Valley, and talked as much as possible with the white settlers, and notwithstanding the desire of the latter to see troops brought into requisition, yet some of them don't wish to part with the Indians; nor can they state more than one case in which a Flathead has committed a crime against a white person, and this was the shooting of a cow by one who received one hundred and fifty lashes for the offence by order of the chief Charlos."

Three years; Charlos still holds out. Here is a quiet scheme to dispossess him:

" There are yet between 300 and 400 Flatheads living in that valley, adherents of the chief Charlos, who so far have refused to listen to any counsel for removal, and hold no communication with the agency whatever; having apparently abandoned all relations with the Government, believing that the Garfield treaty will never be fully carried out. However, as an order has been issued by the county authorities for the assessment of their property with the view of collecting taxes, the majority of them will, if the Garfield promises are kept in good faith before them, probably remove to the Jocko within another year."

It must be borne in mind that the Indians were wholly without the protection of law, with no standing in the courts, and no vote or other representation of any kind. An Indian was not even declared to be a *person* in the eyes of the law until 1879. Now if there is one principle of government that does *not* find a place in the boasted declarations of the Free and Equal, it is that of taxation without representation. How will a scheme so un-American be received at the seat of Government?

The Honorable Commissioner of Indian Affairs, in his report for that year to the Honorable Secretary of the Interior, says:

" The remaining 350 Flatheads, under two chiefs, are still in the Bitter Root Valley, and hold no communication with the agency, and are trying to maintain themselves on their farms. Whether they will prove equal to the competition which the settlements have brought around them, and be able to save their property from sheriff's sale by prompt payment of taxes, is yet a question. Amid the eager desire to gain possession of their valuable farms, there will be few days of grace after the taxes are due."

It is a curious coincidence that at this time the country was celebrating the one hundredth anniversary of its own famous protest against this same form of oppression. "Taxation without representation is tyranny," declared the patriot fathers, and several hundred chests of taxed tea cast upon the waters of Boston Harbor proclaimed their sentiment in concrete terms. So, at this centennial time, the Government looked approvingly upon the festivities of its Chosen, while it calmly discussed the same scheme of taxation for another distressed people — not for revenue only, but as a means to gain the property taxed.

Five years; the confiscation scheme seems to have failed:

"The whole Flathead tribe, consisting of nearly four hundred souls, with the exception of the few families who removed to this agency, adhere to Charlos and follow his fortunes, choosing rather to eke out a livelihood by their own exertions in the neighborhood of their venerated chief than to accept the bounty of the Government and leave their homes. . . ."

The summer of 1877 was an eventful one in the mountains of the Northwest. A portion of the Nez Perces in Idaho, under Chief Joseph, refused the demand of the Government for the evacuation of their valley and location on a reservation. Troops were hurried to the valley, and the command to move was repeated with a show of force. This led to murder, and murder to war. The Nez Perces, flee-

ing before the United States troops under General
O. O. Howard, came directly through the Bitter
Root Valley. They called upon their old friends,
the Flatheads, to join their cause. Could a tribe
of harassed Indians resist this appeal?

The Jocko agent reports: " They not only refrained
from joining their ancient allies, the Nez Perces, but
they gave them warning that if an outrage was
committed, either to the person or property of any
settler of the Bitter Root Valley, in their retreat
before General Howard's advancing troops, they
would immediately make war upon them; and to
this worthy action of Charlos, the non-treaty Flathead chief, and the chiefs and head-men of this
reservation, do the white settlers of the Bitter Root
Valley owe their preservation of life and property
during those trying days."

Now it would seem possible for a great Government to be magnanimous in a case of this kind
without offending petty politicians; under similar
circumstances one might expect something handsome
from the king of the Hottentots. A communication
from the agent to the Commissioner contains the
story of the Indians' reward:

" . . . The Flatheads lost their crops, owing in
part to neglect, caused by assisting the whites in
guarding their homes, and to a hail-storm which
cut everything down before it that season, leaving
them destitute, and compelling them to go to the

buffalo country to sustain life by the chase, as they were refused any assistance by the government, although I made an earnest appeal in their behalf at the time."

Seven years; the lines are drawing closer:

"Under Chief Charlos some 350 Flatheads still cling to their homes in the Bitter Root Valley, refusing to remove to this reservation. The rapid settling up of the valley by a white population has hedged these people in so closely that there is scarcely grazing room for their cattle and horses."

A new scheme now comes to light. The Indians were induced — by misrepresentations which will appear — to sign a request for patents of the tracts of land occupied by them individually as farms. Of course, the acceptance of such patents would be equivalent to a surrender of the entire valley, with the exception of the little tracts on which they actually lived.

But the abandonment of " the Bitter Root Valley, above the Lo-Lo Fork," which Charlos steadfastly insisted must be " set apart as a separate reservation for said tribe," was far from the Indian intention. They were shrewd enough to perceive the significance of the plan when the patents were offered to them. The agent reports:

"Charlos, the chief, refused to accept his patent, and of course all the Indians present followed his example. In explanation he said, in substance, that the treaty agreed upon between his father, Victor, head chief of the Flathead nation, and other Indian chiefs, and Governor Stevens on the part of the Government, on the 16th of July, 1855, provided that the Bitter Root Valley, above the Lo-Lo Fork, should be set apart as a separate reservation for the Flathead tribe. . . .

"In regard to the issue of the patents, Charlos claims that that matter was never properly explained to him or his people, and when they gave their names for title *they simply understood they were signing a petition to the President to allow them to retain the Bitter Root Valley as a separate reservation* from the Jocko, as agreed upon by the eleventh article of the treaty. I found it in vain to try to explain the precise meaning and wording of this clause, as he persisted that it was the Indian understanding that according to the Stevens [Victor] treaty they have a valid right and title to the Bitter Root Valley as a reservation. It was also inferred by him that if his people did accept the patents they would not know where to find the land, as a part of what he claimed to be his land has already been taken away from him by a white man, who claimed his land ran through it. Taxation and the breaking up of tribal relations is another objection, and also an utter lack of appreciation or confidence in the good intentions of the Government. He fully appreciates the strength of the Government and the fact that he can be forced into measures, but he claims that if it should come to that he will only ask the privilege to seek another home in another country of his own choice rather than give up his title to the Bitter Root as a reservation by accepting a patent for his farm or by removing to the Jocko.

"I would state to the honorable Commissioner that the affairs of the Flatheads of the Bitter Root Valley are in a most deplorable and unsatisfactory condition, and my motive in entering into so many details is to place the matter before you in as intelligent form as I can, so that some action may be taken to settle the question definitely without resort to force. The time is surely approaching when the Bitter Root land question will lead to serious difficulty, as the valley is fast being settled by thrifty farmers. The chief, Charlos, is a good and peaceable Indian, and well respected by the whites, but he clings to the notion that his people have been wronged in regard to the Bitter Root question."

Twelve years; Charlos still gazes fondly upon the land of his fathers, and awaits with childlike faith the fulfilment of the promise "if it shall prove, in the judgment of the President, to be better adapted to the wants of the Flathead tribe." The agent suggested to the Department the advisability of "inviting Charlos to a conference at Washington, when the intentions of the Government for the welfare of his people might be thoroughly impressed upon him." Charlos went to see the " Great Father." The record of that visit is interesting:

" In January, 1884, Chief Charlos and four of his head-men, accompanied by the agent and an interpreter, visited Washington under orders from the Indian Department. Nearly a month was spent at the National Capitol, and during that time several interviews were held with the Secretary of the Interior, but no offer of pecuniary reward or persuasion of the Secretary could shake Charlos' resolution to remain in the Bitter Root Valley. An offer to build him a house, fence in and plough a sufficiency of land for a farm, give him cattle, horses, seed, agricultural implements, and to do likewise for each head of a family in his band; also a yearly pension to Charlos of $500, and [to] be recognized as the heir of Victor, his deceased father, and to take his place as head chief of the confederated tribes of Flatheads, Pend d'Oreilles, and Kootenais Indians, living on the Jocko reservation, had no effect."

On one hand, poverty, the white man's promise, and the home of his people; on the other, plenty, and the Jocko. Charlos' grip on the national pledge could not be loosened; his country was not for sale. And Charlos seems to have considered himself " the heir of Victor, his deceased father," regardless of Washington's approval or consent.

Having failed to liquidate the national obligation in

The Story of the Bitter Root

open conference with Charlos, the Honorable Secretary devised a new plan of campaign:

"In compliance with verbal instructions from the Honorable Secretary of the Interior, a full report of which I furnished the Indian Office under date of March 27, 1884, I made certain propositions to individual families to remove from the Bitter Root and settle at the Flathead reservation, and the result was that twenty-one heads of families concluded to remove, and to them, following the views of the Honorable Secretary of the Interior, as expressed to the Indians in Washington, I promised to each (1) a choice of 160 acres of unoccupied land on the reservation; (2) the erection of a suitable house; (3) assistance in fencing and breaking up ten acres of land for each family; (4) the following gifts: two cows, a wagon, set of harness, a plough, with other agricultural implements, seed for the first year, and provisions until the first crop was harvested."

Quite tempting inducements, surely. It may be interesting to know what sort of Indians these seceders were; the agent supplies the information:

"The members of Charlos' band who removed from the Bitter Root to this agency cannot be classed among the most industrious and civilized members of the tribe. In fact the colony is composed mostly of Indians who, with their families, followed the buffalo until this game became almost extinct, and continued to make a precarious living by hunting, fishing, and wandering among the settlements."

Fourteen years; more of the band have given up the struggle. Three hundred and forty-one remain in the Bitter Root Valley.

Fifteen years; the pressure is telling on Charlos' followers. The agent writes: "Those who choose to remain should be made to understand that they need look no further for Government aid;" and the number drops to two hundred and seventy-eight.

Sixteen years; Charlos and one hundred and eighty-nine still cling to their forlorn hope.

Seventeen years; now one hundred and seventy-six. But the census of the confederated tribes on the Jocko shows a *decrease* of one hundred and four. The Indians seem in truth to be going to a " better country."

Eighteen years; still one hundred and seventy-six. But a handful of men cannot hold out forever against a government intent on their peaceful reduction. Denied the protection of the courts against the encroachment of the whites, they were finally reduced to a condition of abject poverty. The time was at hand when the interests of humanity, in the absence of original justice, demanded that these people be wrested from the land they loved too well. At this opportune time a proposition was made to sell their lands and improvements and devote the proceeds to their establishment on the Jocko. The terms were accepted, and in 1890, after eighteen years of endeavor as an independent people, maintaining to the last the peace they had promised to General Garfield, Charlos and his band surrendered their beloved valley of the Bitter Root.

Such a surrender arouses a mingled feeling of relief and added interest. Of relief, for the vanquished are no more under the stern displeasure that has borne them down; of added interest, for it brings opportunity to a magnanimous victor.

This is the record in the Great Book:

" The last arrangement with this unfortunate band and the delay in its consummation has entirely discouraged the Indians. They are now helpless and poverty-stricken on their land in that valley, looking forward to the promise for the sale of lands patented to certain members of that band and to their removal to this reservation. The hope was given them, when their consent was secured for an appraisement and sale of their lands and improvements, that arrangements would be made to remove them to the Jocko reservation before the 1st of March, 1890, in order to give them an opportunity to select lands on the reserve and to put in crops to harvest this year. With that view they could not be induced to plough or sow their land in the Bitter Root Valley. They are destitute of means of support and, if the contemplated appropriation to remove and support them until they can raise crops is not carried out this year, some means should be adopted to furnish them with provisions, or they will certainly suffer from starvation."

The Indians were in fact not removed until the autumn of the following year. It seems beyond belief that indifference for the welfare of this tribe should have followed so closely upon their giving up the coveted valley, but for some inexplicable reason the money received from the sale of their farms was withheld for three years more, although $14,674.53 were reported on hand in 1892, nearly two years before the first payment was made to them. In 1893 the agent reports:

" These Indians are very anxious in regard to the payment to them of the money already paid to the Government from sale of certain tracts of said lands, claiming that it was promised to be sent without delay for distribution to the owners or heirs of the same, in order to enable them to improve and cultivate their new farms on their reservation."

The record discloses nothing that accounts for this situation. It deals with facts, not explanations. But we find these once independent farmers on a bare reservation, without means to begin life anew, reduced to the condition of ration Indians, living for four years on the bounty of the Government. The voice of Charlos is raised in one continued

The Story of the Bitter Root

protest; but even this man of indomitable will seems to have reached the limit of his endurance, and it is painful to find him at last embittered, broken in spirit, with little faith in the white man and his ways.

Finally, four years after their surrender of the Bitter Root, the first payment arrived:

"This payment was made at a most opportune time in the early spring. The money was paid by check, but the following day all the beneficiaries proceeded by rail to Missoula, where, in the presence of the agent, their checks were cashed, and though the sum paid was over $18,000, and the number of Indians receiving shares was 47, not one of their number could be tempted by the numerous whiskey vendors, and all, after making some purchases of tools, implements, clothing, and provisions, returned quietly to their reservation."

Here we leave Charlos and his heroic band. Charlos — an ignorant, unknown Indian. But in patriotic endeavor for his people according to his light; in steadfast love of liberty, justice, and native land, he shared in the nobility of some with whom the Fates have dealt more kindly. A once struggling people are pleased to call such a man the Father of his country.

It is the story of an endeavor that failed. The Bitter Root Valley was added to the land of the Noble Free, at a cost in money insignificant compared with its value; but in the pledging of the national faith, " if it shall prove, in the judgment of the President, to be better adapted to the wants of the Flathead tribe," have they not paid the price incalculable — the national honor?

THE NEZ PERCES

"The line was made as I wanted it; not for me, but my children that will follow me; there is where I live, and there is where I want to leave my body. The land on the other side of the line is what we gave to the Great Father." Joseph, Nez Perce Chief.

WITH many words of friendship the Nez Perce chiefs, speaking in Indian council forty-five years ago, hailed the long-delayed ratification of the treaty which gave to the white man the Nez Perce country, and to the Nez Perces an Indian reservation within it.

Four years before — in 1855 — the treaty had been signed by the chiefs and head-men of the Nez Perce nation in council with Governor Stevens, of Washington, and Governor Palmer, of Oregon. The reservation secured to the Indians was of generous proportions. It included the principal valleys occupied by the different bands, or tribes, of the nation, and the hardship of severing their connection with native land fell upon very few of the Nez Perces. "Nor shall any white man," the treaty recites, "excepting those in the employment of the Indian Department, be permitted to reside upon the said reservation without permission of the tribe and the superintendent and agent." In consideration for the cession of territory, the Nez Perces were to have annuities, schools, blacksmiths, carpenters, farmers, a sawmill, and a gristmill; the head chief, a very politic old Indian named "Lawyer," found himself — in the treaty — provided with a furnished house and five hundred dollars a year. This was designated by courtesy as "salary." Head chiefs in more highly organized society have been propitiated in much the same way.

It was a most liberal treaty; and it was good policy to make a liberal treaty with these most numerous and powerful of all the mountain Indians, especially in view of the fierce rush for gold that had maddened the Indian tribes of the great Northwest to the verge of war. During that year Governors Stevens and Palmer made treaties with many of the tribes, under instructions from Washington, to extinguish the Indian title to the gold region and gather the natives upon reservations.

The subsequent history of the Northwest would have been less bloody, less filled with tales of Indian massacres and Indian wars, had the Government fulfilled with any degree of promptness its obligations; but Congress, year after year, failed to render the treaties operative by ratifying them, while the Indians, accepting in good faith the terms of their agreements, vacated the ceded lands and gathered upon the tracts reserved for them, to await the benefits that were promised in the way of annuities, instruction, and implements of agriculture.

The Nez Perces

They waited in vain. Deprived as they were of their hunting-grounds and the only means of subsistence, starvation and the inhuman treatment of the miners soon drove them to desperation; the records are full of their pleadings with Government agents to give them relief.

"I am not a bad man," says Seattle, a great chief in western Washington, "I am, and always have been, a friend to the whites. I listen to what Mr. Paige says to me, and I do not steal, nor do I or any of my people kill the whites.

"Oh, Mr. Simmons, why don't our papers come back to us? You always say you hope they will soon come, but they do not. I fear we are forgotten, or that we are to be cheated out of our land.

"I have been very poor and hungry all winter, and am very sick now [a fact]. In a little while I will die. I should like to be paid for my land before I die. Many of my people died during the last cold, scarce winter, without getting their pay.

"When I die my people will be very poor. They will have no property, no chief, no one to talk for them. You must not forget them, Mr. Simmons, when I am gone.

"We are ashamed when we think that the Puyallups have their papers. They fought against the whites, while we, who have never been angry with them, get nothing."

The Indian Dispossessed

And this from a Snohomish chief:

"We want our treaty to be concluded as soon as possible; we are tired of waiting. Our reasons are that our old people (and there are many of them) are dying. Look at those two old men and old women; they have only a little while to live, and they want to get their pay for their land. The white people have taken it, and you, Mr. Simmons, promised us that we should be paid. You and Governor Stevens. Suspense is killing us. We are afraid to plant potatoes on the river bottoms, lest some bad white man should come and make us leave the place.

"You know what we are, Mr. Simmons. You were the first American we ever knew, and our children remember you as long as they remember anything. I was a boy when I first knew you. You know we do not want to drink liquor, but we cannot help it when the bad 'Bostons' bring it to us.

"When our treaty was made we told our hearts to you and Governor Stevens; they have not changed since. I have done."

There is a significant interest in this one:

"I will now talk about our treaties. When is the Great Father that lives across the far mountains going to send us our papers back? Four summers have now passed since you and Governor Stevens told us we would get pay for our land. We remember well what you said to us then, over there

The Nez Perces

[pointing to Point Elliott], and our hearts are very sick because you do not do as you promised. We saw the Nisquallys and Puyallups get their annuity paid them last year, and our hearts were sick because we could get nothing. We never fought the whites; they did. If you whites pay the Indians that fight you, it must be good to fight."

"*It must be good to fight.*" Slowly the Indians came into a full understanding of the "hopelessly illogical" policy of the Government under which its benefits were "proportioned not to the good but to the ill desert of the several tribes." War and desolation filled the land, and the tribes of the mountains stubbornly maintained an unequal struggle for that which, to their untutored minds, seemed to be their own country. A despairing and pathetic contest it is when an unlettered race, with its simple views of fundamental justice, comes against calculating, enlightened, and overwhelming might; the dim realization of inferiority kindles in the benighted mind a desperate ferocity which is akin to patriotic zeal in more civilized defenders of native land.

It is impossible to account for this policy of inaction. Millions more were spent in these wars than would have met every obligation under the treaties. Superintendents, agents, and army officers in the field sent appeal after appeal to the Government to act upon the treaties and stop the useless destruction.

The Indian Dispossessed

One agent, sending in the pleas of several still friendly Indian chiefs, writes:

"After reading this I think that you, sir, must agree with me in thinking that humanity, as well as justice, makes it an imperative duty of Government to adopt some plan by which the Indians can be separated from the whites. Their forbearance has been remarkable. While they had the power of crushing us like worms they treated us like brothers. We, I think, should return their kindness now that we have the power, and our duty is so plainly pointed out by their deplorable situation. My own impression is that the speediest and best way of settling all these difficulties is the ratification of the treaties. The agents will then have the means in their hands of supplying all that I now think is wanting to enable them to govern these unhappy creatures, and to lay the groundwork of civilization for their children to improve upon."

An officer in the field calls the attention of the Honorable Commissioner of Indian Affairs with no mincing of words to the labors of Stevens and Palmer:

"Those seeing these things at a still later day, and being in position to avert them by a wise, discreet policy for ourselves, and a just one for the Indian, set to work, and from the Rocky Mountains to the Pacific coast labored hard and long in the field and office, travelling through every Indian tribe, learning their history and wants, and with the au-

78

thoritative voice of the Government made three years ago treaties with these Northwestern Indians, and to this day the labors of Governor Stevens are disregarded and uncared for, and the treaties containing the solemn promises of the Indian on the one side, and binding obligations of the Government on the other, lie among the dusty archives of Congress, while a war rages in every quarter of the Northwest coast. The Indians feel that their rights have been trifled with by promises, made by agents armed and vested with authority to act, which the Government has not ratified. And will it, I ask, longer remain in this passive mood? Will it longer act inertly while lives are sacrificed and millions squandered, and still longer hesitate to act? For one I trust not. Let these be ratified. . . ."

In the command of this officer was a company of thirty Nez Perce warriors, who, the record recites, "marshalling themselves under brave war chiefs, were placed at his disposal to assist him in finding and fighting his enemy." Writing of the Nez Perce tribe, this officer says:

"This is the same people who, meeting the flying columns of Colonel Steptoe in hot night-retreat, having abandoned animals, provisions, and guns behind them, received him with open arms, succored his wounded men, and crossed in safety his whole command over the difficult and dangerous south fork of the Columbia. . . .

The Indian Dispossessed

" They are far advanced already in civilization —
much further than any tribe west of the Rocky
Mountains, except the Flatheads. They are inclined
to agriculture; already raise wheat, corn, and vegetables, with the rudest of means. When asked by
Colonel Wright what they wanted, their reply was
well worthy of a noble race: '*Peace, ploughs, and
schools.*' And will you, can you, longer refuse them
these? I ask, therefore, to commend these noble
people. Colonel Wright has given me the command
of this band of warriors while in the field, and
hence I am in a position to know and study them.
I ask that a special appropriation be made to give
these people schools, farms, and seeds; that means
be taken to so build them up in their mountain
homes that we may be enabled to point with joy-
ous pride to a first few tutored savages reclaimed
from their wild, nomadic habits; and while asking,
aye petitioning, for these, I cannot forget my old
mountain friends the Flatheads and Pend d'Oreilles.
As yet they are friendly, and I ask that you retain
their friendship. I made both to Governor Stevens
and to yourself, four year ago, petitions in their
favor; but, alas! they passed unheeded. I again
renew them, and ask that steps, prompt and efficient,
be taken that will avert from these noble bands the
devastating arm of war. I ask not that my version
be taken alone, but simply ask that it go to form
part and parcel of versions given by abler pens, and

The Nez Perces

men who saw but to reflect upon the past and future destiny of the Indians. I point you, commencing with Lewis and Clark in 1804 to the present day, to the accounts of all travellers across the continent; and with one accord they point to the Nez Perces and Flatheads as two bright, shining points in a long and weary pilgrimage across a prairie desert and rugged mountain barrier, alive with savage hordes of Indians, where they have been relieved and aided when most in need; and instances sufficiently numerous to swell a volume exist, that render it needless for me here to refer to them. But I make one more appeal in behalf of these people."

Chief Lawyer joined in the general appeal with a diplomatic reminder, addressed to Governor Stevens:

"At this place about three years since we had our talk, and since that time I have been waiting to hear from our Big Father. We are very poor. It is other people's badness. It is not our fault, and I would like to hear what he has to say. If he thinks our agreement good, our hearts will be thankful.

"Colonel Wright has been over after the bad people, and has killed some of the bad people and hung sixteen; and now I am in hopes we will have peace."

This the Governor at once sent to the Commissioner in Washington, with an appeal for the ratification of their treaty.

In 1859 the wars ended, as all Indian wars end,

with the last hostile tribe " reduced to the condition of suppliants for charity." Throughout the four years the Nez Perces, Flatheads, and Pend d'Oreilles remained steadfast friends of the whites, and the ratification of their treaties came as a long-delayed reward.

A Government agent bore the news to the expectant Nez Perces, and a grand council was called to welcome the word from their Great Father. Lawyer, the head chief, Joseph, Looking-glass, and numerous sub-chiefs, voiced their hearty approval of their new relation to the Great Father in Washington; in the characteristic Indian way they expressed their gratitude, their firm determination to maintain a perpetual peace, their blind confidence in the stability of the new covenant. The record of this council is quite complete.

Lawyer, head chief of the Nez Perces nation, made the opening speech:

" I heard you talk yesterday. I heard what the Great Father said. He has laws for his white children and for his red children. He says: ' My white children must do what is right, and my red children must do the same; that is the law.'

" The Great Father tells us his heart through you, and now you have told us all he has to say; it is good. Your law for us is right. I respect the law; my children and young men respect it.

" Now, I will tell you my heart; the chiefs are

here, and I want them to listen to me. I don't want any of my chiefs and young men to harm the whites; we always were friends, are now and always will be; you all know my heart, it is to do right. That is all I have to say."

Looking-glass, a sub-chief in Joseph's tribe, then spoke:

"I am now going to say to you what I said to Governor Stevens, four years ago. I told him the amount of country I wanted, and where it laid, and also what I wanted it for. Governor Stevens said yes. That is all I said in council. Our treaty was sent to the Great Father, and he answers it now. He says yes; his word has come. It is the same as if I had seen the great father and exchanged hearts with him. He says he wants my children to do well; he will take care of them. He talks of this country. I want all of you to talk; all of my young men to talk. I am thankful for the word the Great Father has sent us."

And another:

"E-YEM-MO-MO-KIN. Yes, my friends, I heard my name called yesterday, on the list of signers of the treaty. Now, I am going to talk. I am an old man; you told us yesterday that we old men will die on our own lands, and I thank you, my white friend. I am glad to hear from our Great Father, and to know that he will provide for our children that will follow us. It makes my heart good.

The Indian Dispossessed

"I want them to take hold of hands and never let go. We have taken your hands, my white friend, and I hope we will never part. I have heard the Lawyer and others talk, and my heart is the same as theirs."

Joseph, chief of the Nez Perces in the Wallowa Valley, delivered the most serious and thoughtful speech of them all. Looking into the future, as his fellow-chiefs evidently did not, he saw in the white man's protection the loss of Indian control, of tribal restraint, and in the loose communism of the reservation he saw the danger to the individual. Joseph saw these things darkly, instinctively; his untutored mind could grasp only the immediate needs of his people; but the breaking down of tribal restraints without the substitution of adequate law, and the herding together of a heterogeneous mass in a communism of idleness with the consequent destruction of individual incentive, have been solely responsible for the fearful degeneracy of the reservation Indian during the past forty years. In Joseph's words there is a wisdom that he knew not of; his earnest plea for the Indian's individuality is of deep significance:

"I want to tell you my heart. I am a red man. I have my own opinion about this country; we should make up our minds before we talk. When we made a treaty with Governor Stevens, the line was drawn; I know where it is; you told us right yesterday; it is as you said. When Governor Stevens made the

84

Nez Perce Camp on the Yellowstone

(1871)

line, he wanted a certain chain of mountains. I said no, I wanted it to hunt in, not for myself, but for my children; but my word was doubted.

"The line was made as I wanted it; not for me, but my children that will follow me; there is where I live, and there is where I want to leave my body. The land on the other side of the line is what we gave to the Great Father.

"You told us yesterday if there is anything we do not understand, you will explain. I will tell you one thing; I have a great many bad young men. I don't want them all to live together in one place; it will not do. We have too many horses and cattle to feed on one piece of land; and I am afraid that my young men and young men of other parties will not get along together. I don't only talk so to-day, but I will tell you the same some other time. We will talk this matter over some other time.

"My young men get drunk, quarrel, and fight, and I don't know how to stop it. A great many of my men have been killed by it; and I am afraid of liquor.

"I think we cannot all live in one place; it is better for each tribe to live in their own country. We will talk of this matter some other time.

"This summer some of my children were mixed up with other tribes, and some of them done wrong; and if the buildings you spoke of, and are mentioned in the treaty, were divided, it would be better for us all. I have told you my mind as it is. I wish you could arrange it so we could live in our own country. I know my young men are wild, and it is better to keep them separated. It is better for all to live as we are. That is all I have to say."

The agent was impressed: " I have heard Joseph talk," he responded, " and my heart is glad. His talk is that of a wise man." Joseph prevailed, and the different tribes maintained their separate existence, each in its native valley, but still within the limits of the reservation; in the words of the Honorable Commissioner of Indian Affairs, " Chief Lawyer occupying the Kamiah Valley, Big Thunder the Lapwai, Timothy the Alpowai, Joseph the Wallowa, and Billy the Salmon River Valley."

In his report of this council with the Nez Perces, the agent says:

" This tribe, who have been the friends of the whites since the visit of Lewis and Clark to the country, having protected and saved the lives of Governor Stevens and his party, in 1855; organized a party who served with Colonel Wright during his campaign against the hostiles last year; and during every exigency where the whites have needed friends, they have been their firm allies, and [are] entitled to great consideration on the part of Government."

But subsequent happenings give this paragraph a peculiar interest:

" I found there had been great dissatisfaction, not in regard to the treaty, but from the circula-

TA-MA-SON = TIMOTHY, — NEZ PERCE

(1871)

tion of false rumors amongst them by renegades from other tribes, to the effect that they were being deluded with the idea that their ' treaty ' was good, and would be carried out *until the whites and soldiers were strong enough to take their lands by force.*"

The meddlers may have been " renegades "; but in making this prediction they were wizards, soothsayers.

Scarcely had the Nez Perces settled down under the treaty to learn the white man's way, when the discovery of gold brought a rush of miners and adventurers into the reservation itself. No effort seems to have been made to restrain them, and the provision in the covenant, " nor shall any white man . . . be permitted to reside upon said reservation," became a dead letter. Indeed, the whole energy of the interested white population was directed toward securing another curtailment of the Indians' country. Year by year the situation grew worse; the official story is briefly told by the Commissioner of Indian Affairs in a report to the Secretary of the Interior:

" In defiance of law, and despite the protestations of the Indian agent, a town site was laid off in October, 1861, on the reservaton, and Lewiston, with a population of twelve hundred, sprung into existence. . . .

" By the spring of 1863 it was very evident that, from the change of circumstances and contact with the whites, a new treaty was required to properly define and, if possible, curtail the limits of the reserve."

"To properly define and, if possible, curtail the limits of the reserve." A most diplomatic phrase; the Honorable Commissioner was writing for public perusal. To "properly define," primarily, and to "curtail," incidentally, a new treaty was required. Diplomacy never more delicately screened a real intention behind a fictitious one. No time was wasted in defining the limits of the reserve; the white men knew where they were; the Indians understood them; nobody misunderstood them. A new treaty was drawn up, cutting down the reservation to a plat of land about one-eighth of its original size, in the centre of the old reserve. Then came the usual struggle to gain the Indian assent. The Wallowa Valley was excluded under the new treaty, and Joseph refused to sign it; Looking-glass, White Bird, and many other chiefs whose country was to be taken from them, refused to sign. Even Lawyer, the head chief, whose country in the Kamiah was to be made the centre of the many benefits to come from the new treaty, held out long against the humiliating cut to "twenty acres each" of tillable land for each adult male. But the treaty is full of "Kamiah," although the agency was at Lapwai. "Ten thousand dollars for the erection of a saw and flouring mill, to be located at Kamiah"; a church "on the Kamiah"; a blacksmith shop "at

The Nez Perces

Kamiah "; Lawyer's " salary " was continued, and a like " salary " to two of his sub-chiefs, " who shall assist him in the performance of his public services "; six hundred dollars more to another of his chiefs, " in consideration of past services and faithfulness "; and Lawyer signed — " with fifty other chiefs and head-men, twenty of whom were parties to the treaty of 1855," records the Commissioner.

Fifty-eight chiefs and headmen had signed the original treaty eight years before; only twenty of these fifty-eight signed the new treaty. Now, where were the missing thirty-eight who did not sign? And again, whence arose *thirty* new chiefs and head-men in so short a time, to sign the new treaty?

This is not the only time that, while a treaty waited, chiefs and head-men were made to order to meet the demand for signers.

With these fifty signatures the treaty was declared to be the expression of a majority of the Nez Perce nation, and all outside tribes were given one year in which to come within the limits of the new reservation. It is impossible to perceive either honesty or justice in thus getting a favored portion of an Indian nation to sign away the possessions of outside tribes, who were holding their native valleys under express agreement with their Great Father in Washington. A few of the outside Indians bowed to the inevitable, and removed to the reserve, but the majority did not; Joseph, always tenacious of the Indian right to lead the Indian life, refused to move; he continued in possession of the Wallowa Valley.

The Nez Perce nation became divided against itself; two factions, "treaty" and "non-treaty" Indians, were the direct result of the new treaty.

From the very beginning of their reservation life the Nez Perces were the victims of more than the usual amount of official pilfering, and a persistent reluctance on the part of their "Great Father" to fulfil his treaty obligations added to their suspicion that to "take hold of hands and never let go" might mean either a token of perpetual peace or of perpetual bondage.

To such limits was the robbery carried that in 1862 — the year before the new treaty — the entire force of the agency was discharged, and the superintendent made a personal investigation. This is what he found:

"I sought in vain to find the first foot of land fenced or broken by him and his employees, and the only product of the agricultural department that I could discover consisted of some three tons of oats in the straw, piled up within a rude, uncovered enclosure of rails, to raise which must have cost the Government more than seven thousand dollars. Even this property was barely saved by the present agent from the hands of the departing employees, who claimed it as the result of their private labor.

The Nez Perces

" As I witnessed the withdrawal from this meagre pile of the rations for my horse, I could hardly fail to sigh to think that every movement of his jaws devoured at least a dollar's worth of governmental bounty.

" The chiefs whom I met in council complained that the employees heretofore sent to instruct them under the provisions of the treaty had taken their women to live with, and had done little else; and they seemed desirous to know if that was the method proposed by the Government to carry out the stipulations of the treaty.

" Several of these discharged employees were lounging around the agency waiting for their female Indian companions to receive their proportion of the annuity goods."

But it makes little difference to the Indian whether the agent gets his goods and confiscates them, or the goods are not furnished at all by the Government. Such fine reasoning as " insufficient appropriations " or " delays incident to change of administration " is not within the scope of the Indian mind. He knows only that he does not receive his just dues, and with simple Indian directness he refuses to entertain excuses in lieu of annuities. In 1866 the Nez Perces were still dreaming of the alluring benefits which were to come to them under their second treaty:

" The Indians of southern Idaho are fast fading away, and as we occupy their root grounds, converting them into fields and pastures, we must either protect them or leave them to the destroying elements now surrounding them, the result of which cannot be doubtful. A humane magnanimity dictates their protection and speedy separation from those evils to which they are exposed by intermingling with white men.

" Prominent among the tribes of northern Idaho stand the Nez Perces, a majority of whom boast that they have ever been the faithful friend of the white man. But few over half of the entire tribes of the Nez Perces are under treaty. The fidelity of those under treaty, even under the most discouraging circumstances, must commend itself to the favorable consideration of the department. The influx of the white population into their country has subjected them to all the evils arising from an association with bad white men, and, as might well be expected, the effect upon the Indians has been most unhappy. The non-payment of their annuities has had its natural effect upon the minds of some of those under treaty; but their confiding head chief (Lawyer) remains unmoved, and on all occasions is found the faithful apologist for any failure of the Government."

This is the view of the Governor of Idaho. The Nez Perces agent expresses himself freely:

" One great cause of the disagreement and split among this people is the non-payment of their annuities. The non-treaty side throw it up to the other side that now they have sold their country and have got nothing but promises which are being received from year to year, that their annuities will never be here. They use it, too, with such good effect that every day their side is increasing in strength. Many of the young men, and some of the old ones of the Lawyer side, say it is true, and that they had rather be with the non-treaty side and not expect anything than to remain with the Lawyer side and have, every few days, these promises repeated to them. Too much praise cannot be awarded Lawyer, the head chief of the nation, for his endeavors to keep peace between his people and the whites, and to account to them for the want of good faith on the part of the Government. . . .

"It is uphill work for an agent to manage his Indians well when he refers them to certain treaty stipulations reserved as their part, when they can retort by saying that but few of the stipulations on the part of the Government are kept."

Very little good the combined protest did. In the following year the Governor says:

"Their grievances are urged with such earnestness, that even 'Lawyer,' who has always been our apologist, has in a measure abandoned his pacific policy, and asks boldly that we do them justice. From all the facts obtained, it is apparent that had the Government been prompt and just in its dealings with them, it would have given much power and prestige to the treaty party of the Nez Perces, and

The Indian Dispossessed

[have] had a powerful influence in drawing the non-treaty party into the covenant. Even now it may not be too late, but if neglected, war may be reasonably expected. Should the Nez Perces strike a blow, all over our Territory and around our boundaries will blaze the signal fires and gleam the tomahawks of the savages."

Even the prospect of war failed to arouse Washington to a sense of its treaty obligations. Another change of administration, and a new agent — a second lieutenant in the army — records his first experience as a purveyor of promises:

"I arrived here on the 14th of July, 1869, and assumed the direction of affairs on the 15th. The Indians on hearing of my arrival commenced coming to see me. Among the first that came was 'Lawyer,' the head chief, who seemed to be well pleased that 'General Grant had sent him a soldier chief,' and in the course of the conversation he told me that some of his people had gone to the buffalo country. Here I first learned that there was a 'non-treaty party' among these Indians. The leading men from all parts of the reservation came to see me, and they, both treaty and non-treaty Indians, all of them, seemed to be well pleased that General Grant had sent them a 'soldier chief.'

"My first object was to find out the cause of the disaffection of this roaming band of Indians known as non-treaty Indians. I found that at first there were but comparatively few of them, and they said at the ratification of the treaty that the Government never meant to fulfil its stipulations; that the white man had no good heart, etc.

"And as time passed on these assertions were verified to some extent by the failure on the part of the Government to build the churches, school-houses, mills at Kamiah, and fence and plough their lands, as provided by treaties of 1859 and 1863, until many of the Indians of the treaty side are beginning to feel sore on account of such failure. These arguments are continually being used by the non-treaty party, and are having great weight, being supported as they are by the stubborn facts. . . .

"These Indians boast with great pride that they as a nation never shed a white man's blood, but the Government has, through its agents, been so dilatory in fulfilling its treaty stipulations, and agents have promised so often that all the stipulations of the treaties would soon be fulfilled, and to so little purpose, that these Indians do not believe that an agent can or will tell the truth.

"I told them at Kamiah that I was going to put up their mill for them. They said in reply that other agents had told them so many years ago."

Little wonder that the non-treaty faction flourished. The wonder is that the treaty element continued to live on expectations. Every action — and every inaction — of the Government served to confirm and strengthen Joseph in his love of the independent life, in his contempt for civilization as it was presented to him, in his fine scorn for the Great Father's promises. He was forced by the logic of events to the conviction that there was no sincerity in the white man's covenants. For ten years after the attempt to extinguish their title to the Wallowa Valley Joseph and his people maintained their separate existence, filling the valley with their herds of horses and cattle during the summer, and retiring each fall to the more sheltered Imnaha Valley for the winter, or to the buffalo country east of the mountains for the annual hunt. During all these years, and as old age came upon him, Joseph impressed upon his two sons, In-me-tuja-latk and Olli-cut, the importance of the trust that would devolve upon them to hold for their people the land which he had saved, "not for myself, but for my children." Upon his death In-me-tuja-latk assumed the name of Joseph, and succeeded to the chieftainship. Young Joseph was then a few years past thirty; in temperament, in ability, in the strength of his conviction that the Indian way was the only way for the Indian, he was the counterpart of his father. A description of this man, who was to be the central figure in the tragic events which cost this tribe its native valley, appears in an official report:

"He is in the full vigor of his manhood; six feet tall, straight, well formed, and muscular; his fore-

IN-ME-TUJA-LATK=ECHOING THUNDER.   CHIEF JOSEPH
(1878)

The Nez Perces

head is broad, his perceptive faculties large, his head
well formed, his voice musical and sympathetic, and
his expression usually calm and sedate; when animated, marked and magnetic. His younger brother
[Ollicut] in whose ability he evidently confides —
putting him forward much of the time as his advocate — is two inches taller than himself, equally well
formed, quite as animated, and perhaps more impassioned in speech, though possibly inferior in
judgment."

Joseph came into the chieftainship at a critical
period in the history of his tribe. In the early
seventies white settlers became so numerous and
persistent in their claims to rich portions of the
Wallowa Valley, and pressed upon Washington their
desire for the expulsion of the Indians with such
political force, that in 1873 a commission was sent
into the valley to arrange with the Indians for their
removal. But, contrary to the expectations of the
Vociferous Few who had brought about the agitation, the Commission decided in favor of the Indian
claim to the Wallowa Valley; the Commissioner of
Indian Affairs approved their finding, the Secretary
of the Interior endorsed it, and the President of the
United States made this order:

"EXECUTIVE MANSION, June 16, 1873.
"It is hereby ordered that the tract of country
above described be withheld from entry and settle-

ment as public lands, and that the same be set apart as a reservation for the roaming Nez Perce Indians, as recommended by the Secretary of the Interior and the Commissioner of Indian Affairs.

"U. S. GRANT."

This executive order not only confirmed to Joseph and his band the Wallowa Valley as their reservation; it implied the endorsement by the highest authority of their contention that the valley had not been ceded under the treaty of 1863, and definitely settled the question of their title to the country that was theirs before the advent of white men. But the order aroused the land-seizing population to a pitch of wild indignation; that the President should affirm the Indian right to Indian land so nearly wrested from him by encroachment and trespass was deemed an outrage without precedent. Meetings were held, representatives in Congress were appealed to, and by every possible means they gave vent to their displeasure. Despite the protests of the Indians and in direct violation of the President's order, the settlers remained in the valley, while Joseph and his people struggled to hold their ground with their herds of cattle and horses. Those were troublous days for Joseph, but knowing full well that any retaliation for outrages committed upon the Indians would be hailed by the settlers as a welcome opportunity to annihilate his people, he succeeded in maintaining peace and a fair proportion of his rights in the valley.

In matters vitally affecting the American Indian, there has yet to be recorded a single instance where the vote-seeking Government officials have long withstood the demands of the Vociferous Few. The Governor of Oregon made a strong personal appeal to Washington for the expulsion of the Indians; inspired by the delegation from Oregon, Congress refused to appropriate the necessary funds for the reimbursement and removal of settlers, thus blocking the executive order. And the great Government meekly, humbly bowed before the new state of Oregon. Within two years of the first order, and wholly without notice to Joseph, a second order came from the President's hand:

" EXECUTIVE MANSION, June 10, 1875.

" It is hereby ordered that the order dated June 16, 1873, withdrawing from sale and settlement and setting apart the Wallowa Valley, in Oregon, described as follows: . . . as an Indian reservation, is hereby revoked and annulled, and the said described tract of country is hereby restored to the public domain.

" U. S. GRANT."

By this stroke of the pen the Indians became trespassers in their own country. It became the duty of the agent to acquaint them with this latest change in their relation to the Government:

The Indian Dispossessed

" When I received information from the Department to the effect that the Wallowa Valley had been opened to settlers, I sent for ' Joseph,' and upon his arrival informed him of the same. At the first interview he was inclined to be ugly, and returned to his camp very much dissatisfied with the action of the Government. In the course of a week he came back and talked more reasonably. To guard against any trouble that might arise, I requested General O. O. Howard, commander Department Columbia, to station troops in the valley during the fishing season, which request was complied with. I think the question of the Wallowa Valley ought to be definitely settled. The Indians go there with large bands of horses, from which springs nearly all the trouble between the Indians and settlers, the latter having large herds of stock in the valley also."

This occupation by the soldiery marked the beginning of the end; but Joseph steadfastly refused to vacate the Wallowa Valley. A year passed; then a special commission was appointed to proceed to the Nez Perce country and labor with the redoubtable Joseph. They came, they saw, but they did not conquer:

" A few moments before the appointed hour the head of his well mounted column was seen from the agency, turning a point in the road. With military precision and order it massed itself in front of, but at considerable distance from, the church. As he entered the church with his band it was evident that their ranks were considerably swelled by the addition of other prominent non-treaty Indians, as also by some malcontents among those who acknowledge themselves bound by the treaties. The commission occupied the platform of the church. Joseph and his band, sixty or seventy in number (including malcontents), after an exchange of salutations by himself and a few of his headmen with the commission, took seats upon our left, the treaty-Indians filling the right and centre of the house.

"Brief personal introductions by General Howard followed, who also made to Joseph a plain and concise statement of the peaceful errands and objects of the commission.

"From the first it was apparent that Joseph was in no haste. Never was the policy of masterly inactivity more fully inaugurated. He answered every salutation, compliment, and expression of good will, in kind, and duplicated the quantity. An alertness and dexterity in intellectual fencing was exhibited by him that was quite remarkable. . . .

"When, in answer to suggestions and general inquiry, no grievance was stated, the commission plied him with questions touching his occasional occupation of Wallowa Valley, and the irritations and disturbances consequent thereon with the white settlers, he answered, he had not come to talk about land, and added that these white settlers had first informed him of the appointment of this commission, expressing their belief that on its assembling all these troubles would be settled, and they (the whites) would retire from the valley. In this, and the following interviews, which were long drawn out, one of them continuing into the night, Joseph maintained his right to Wallowa Valley, including, as we understood, the tract of country set apart as a reservation for him and his band, by Executive order dated June 16, 1873. . . .

"The earth was his mother. He was made of the earth and grew up on its bosom. The earth, as his mother and nurse, was sacred to his affections, too sacred to be valued by or sold for silver and gold. He could not consent to sever his affections from the land that bore him. He was content to live upon such fruits as the 'Creative Power' placed within and upon it, and unwilling to barter these and his free habits away for the new modes of life proposed by us. Moreover, the earth carried chieftainship (which the interpreter explained to mean law, authority, or control), and therefore to part with the earth would be to part with himself or with his self-control. He asked nothing of the President. He was able to take care of himself. He did not desire Wallowa Valley as a reservation, for that would subject him and his band to the will of and dependence on another, and to laws not of their own making. He was disposed to live peace-

The Nez Perces

ably. He and his band had suffered wrong rather than do wrong. One of their number was wickedly slain by a white man during the last summer, but he would not avenge his death. But, unavenged by him, the voice of that brother's blood, sanctifying the ground, would call the dust of their fathers back to life, to people the land in protest of this great wrong.

"The serious and feeling manner in which he uttered these sentiments was impressive. He was admonished that in taking this position he placed himself in antagonism to the President, whose government extended from ocean to ocean; that if he held to this position, sooner or later there would come an issue, and when it came, as the weaker party he and his band would go to the wall; that the President was not disposed to deprive him of any just right or govern him by his individual will, but merely subject him to the same just and equal laws by which he himself as well as all his people were ruled."

Day after day the commissioners met with the Nez Perces; their report is filled with the picturesque Indian speeches:

"What I tell you is the truth," declares Joseph. "It is not for us to trade off the land that is not traded off; and, as I said before, it is not marked and should be so left. It is a cause of great grief and trouble to us. When there is no cause there is no reason to be troubled. When we heard the whites say that they came to settle there by authority of a Government officer, our hearts were sick. At that time the whites were very troublesome. I said to them, ' My friends, don't do that way; be quiet; we can't get along that way.' At that time I wrote to Washington. It has been yearly for some time that I have sent word to Washington. I think a great deal of my country. I cannot part with it. At that the whites became angry, and told me that it was not my country. You know that our horses do not graze around by our thoughts. I asked the whites if I ever called them to my country. For what purpose did you come to my home? They have been very troublesome for these years. There the whites killed one of our number. We told them we could not commit a wrong on good land. For the purpose of carrying their point one of them lied. I admit my heart was aroused. . . .

" I did not expect to be talked to again about my country by the whites. I will withhold my country from the whites, nor will I let them take it from me. We are not to be trampled upon and our rights taken from us. The right to the land was ours before the whites came among us; white men set such authority aside. If that course were adopted neither would have chiefs — neither would have rest. It ought to fill you with fear. Wrong has been done us. We will not shed blood. Perhaps a law will be found applicable to the case. Law is not without eyes; hence, friends, listen; we will hold to our chieftainship."

Another adjournment, and another day of Indian oratory; Joseph persists in his attachment to the land of his fathers:

"That which I have great affection for, I have no reason or wish to dispose of; if I did, where would I be? The earth and myself are of one mind. The measure of the land and the measure of our bodies are the same. Say to us, if you can say it, that you were sent by the Creative Power to talk to us. Perhaps you think the Creator sent you here to dispose of us as you see fit. If I thought you were sent by the Creator I might be induced to think you had a right to dispose of me. Do not misunderstand me, but understand me fully with reference to my affection for the land. I never said the land was mine to do with it as I chose. The one who has the right to dispose of it is the one who has created it. I claim a right to live on my land, and accord you the privilege to live on yours."

Suggestive questions met with ready answers:

"Mr. Jerome. Is there any other place where you would like to go?

"Young Joseph. I see no place but the Wallowa Valley. It is my home. Everything grows there in the earth. I do not think so much of the fish.

"Mr. Jerome. Haven't you a stronger affection for *peace* than you have for the land?

The Indian Dispossessed

"Young Joseph. I think with reference to the land. I look upon the land, made as it was, with pleasure. It was made for us, with all its natural advantages. I grew up on it, and took it as it was given to me. As it was created, it was finished with power. There is nothing should supersede it. There is nothing which can outstrip it. It is clothed with fruitfulness. In it are riches given me by my ancestors, and from that time up to the present I have loved the land, and was thankful that it had been given me. I don't wish to be understood as talking about the Lapwai, but the Wallowa. I have set my foot down, and have gone as far as I intend to go. I have already shown to you my mind about the country over there, and you know what I think as well as I do.

"Mr. Jerome. What shall we say to the President when we go back?

"Young Joseph. All I have to say is that I love my country."

Another still more suggestive question from General Howard: "Suppose several thousand men should come from Oregon with arms, what would you do?"

Within a year the troops came upon them from Oregon, with General Howard at their head. How prophetic!

Is there anything of the traditional Indian vengeance in this?

".When I learned they had killed one of my

people, it clothed my heart with fear and trouble. My heart was darkened. I was heart-sick. I looked for relief as out of the question. Nothing would bring back the dead. I told them this. I thought when I heard a commission was coming here we could settle this thing and interchange ideas with good effect. My travelling around in my own country used to be unmolested; I went in happiness and peace. The killing of that Indian caused me to feel that darkness pervaded my heart. I thought, when I heard of this commission, perhaps something will be said in the council that will in a measure heal my heart. When I heard the whites had killed the Indian, I thought perhaps they had not been taught the law. By the whites causing the trouble they were brought up to justice by the law. With reference to the body of the white man who committed the deed I have made up my mind. In whatsoever manner I may think concerning the murderer you will hear of as coming from me; I have come to the conclusion to let him escape and enjoy health, and not take his life for the one he took. I am speaking as though I spoke to the man himself. I do not want anything in payment for the deed he committed. *I pronounce the sentence that he shall live.* I spoke to the murderer and told him I thought a great deal of the land on which he had shed the blood of one of my people. When I saw all the settlers take the murderer's part, though they spoke of bringing him to trial, I told them there was no law in favor of murder. I could see they were all in favor of the murderer, so I told them to leave the country. I told them it was of great importance. You see one of our bodies lying dead. I am not talking idly to you. I cannot leave that country and go elsewhere. . . .

"When the whites did not live in the Wallowa, I grew up there; you see my gray hairs now. I have travelled all its trails. Then there were no whites or fences. I have heard what you have said. I think you can reprimand your people so that they will do better. I have stock ranging perhaps the whole length of the creek. That stock I have traded for. I have been listening to the whites for perhaps twenty years. I have said nothing in this line. My children have shown you friendship, and you have set aside that friendship. That much I show up to you."

Pressed for an explanation of his frequent migrations from the valley, Joseph gives this unique justification:

"Joseph said: There is much snow there. In severe weather we go to Imnaha. There is good hunting there. . . . This one place of living is the same as you whites have among yourselves. When you were born, you looked around and found you lived in houses. You grew up to be large men. At any time you wished to go from any point to another, you went. After making such journey, perhaps you came back to a father. I grew up the same way. Whenever my mind was made up to travel, I went. When I got to be quite a lad, I was clothed with wisdom. My eyes were opened. I did see. I saw tracks going in all directions. I grew up seeing the trail as far as the buffalo country, and saw that my seniors had followed it. As large as the earth is, it serves as a house to live in. Seeing as I said, I concluded the earth was made to live in as well as to travel on. I saw in what kind of houses you lived. I approve of them for your use. Whenever I see houses, I know whites have been there; but it is not for me to demolish them. I have already shown to you that the land is as a bed for me. If we leave it, perhaps for years, we expect it to be ready to receive us when we come back."

But the labors of the commissioners were in vain; Joseph made this final declaration:

" You say come on the reservation. I say I don't come on the reservation. As for the Wallowa Valley, I will settle there in *my own way* and *at my own pleasure*. That is the way my heart is, and if you ask each of my people you will find their hearts the same."

The scene of activity now shifts to the War Department. After much correspondence between Washington and the military of the Northwest, the early spring was determined upon for the final move upon Joseph. In February the Nez Perce agent sent a delegation of " treaty " Indians to the Wallowa Valley with an untimatum to the refractory chief. This is Joseph's reply:

" I have been talking to the whites many years about the land in question, and it is strange they cannot understand me. The country they claim belonged to my father, and when he died it was given to me and my people, and I will not leave it until I am compelled to."

By the 1st of May a strong military force, in command of General O. O. Howard, was approaching the Nez Perce country. The General met Joseph and other non-treaty chiefs for a final parley:

" Friday, the 4th of May, the Indians came together again very much reinforced, part of White Bird's Indians and some others having come in. They go through a similar preliminary ceremonial around the garrison. . . .

" Joseph simply introduced White Bird and his people, stating that they had not seen me before, and that he wished them to understand what was said. White Bird sat demurely in front of me, kept his hat on, and steadily covered his face with a large eagle's wing. . . .

" White Bird's Indians, having come a long distance, were evidently very tired. I thought it was best to allow them to assemble again, with a view of keeping them on the reservation and gathering in others still, and let them have time to talk over what we had told them until I could get my troops in position; . . . so when Joseph asked for a postponement till the morrow, I said: 'Let the Indians take time; let them wait till Monday morning; meanwhile they can talk among themselves.' This gave evident satisfaction, and Monday morning at nine o'clock was fixed for the next meeting."

And the Indians gladly welcomed the three days' delay, while the astute General gathered his forces about them.

But there was no common ground for a parley. The Indians were inclined to discuss the old question of their rights to the valley, while General Howard insisted on an immediate compliance with the order to remove from Wallowa to the reserve. One old Indian, Too-hul-hul-sote, seems to have especially irritated the General:

" ' The law is, you must come to the reservation. The law is made in Washington; we don't make it.' Other positive instructions are repeated. Too-hul-hul-sote answers, ' We never have made any trade. Part of the Indians gave up their land; I never did. The earth is part of my body, and I never gave up the earth.'

" I answer, ' You know very well that the Government has set apart a reservation and that the Indians must go on it. . . .'

The Indian Dispossessed

" White Bird, in a milder manner, said he agreed
with Too-hul-hul-sote. He said if he had been taught
from early years to be governed by the whites, then
he would be governed by the whites. ' The earth
sustains me.' I then turned to the old man, whom
they mean to keep at it, and say: ' Then you do not
promise to comply with the orders?' He answers:
' So long as the earth keeps me, I want to be left
alone; you are trifling with the law of the earth.'
I reply: ' Our old friend does not seem to understand that the question is, Will the Indians come
peaceably on the reservation or do they want me to
put them there by force?'

" He then declares again: ' I never gave the In-
dians authority to give away my land.' I asked:
' Do you speak for yourself?' He answered fiercely:
' The Indians may do what they like, but I am *not*
going on the reservation.' Speaking as sternly as
I could, I said:

" ' That bad advice is what you give the Indians;
on account of it you will have to be taken to the
Indian Territory. Joseph and White Bird seem to
have good hearts, but yours is bad; I will send you
there if it takes years and years. When I heard
you were coming, I feared you would make trouble;
you say you are not a medicine man, but you talk
for them. The Indians can see no good while you
are along; you advise them to resist, to lose all
their horses and cattle, and have unending trouble.

112

The Nez Perces

Will Joseph and White Bird and Looking-glass go with me to look after the land? The old man shall not go; he must stay with Captain Perry.' The Old Dreamer says: 'Do you want to scare me with reference to my body?' I then said I would leave his body with Captain Perry, and called for the captain to take him out of the council.

"He was led out accordingly and kept away till the council broke up."

Too-hul-hul-sote was kept in confinement five days. This summary arrest and removal of their spokesman from what they supposed was a friendly council brought the Indians to a realization of the utter hopelessness of their cause; sadly, reluctantly they yielded to the removal. The chiefs were invited to inspect the reservation and select their location; General Howard records his satisfaction with a stern duty well done:

"Having now secured the object named, by persuasion, constraint, and such a gradual encircling of the Indians by troops as to render resistance evidently futile, I thought my own instructions fulfilled.

"The execution of further details I leave in perfect security to the Indian agent and Captain Perry, whom I put into my place for this work."

Constrained as was their compliance with the order, the Indians proceeded in good faith to gather up their goods, collect their herds, and move toward the reservation. Had it not been for a single untoward incident, the story of the Nez Perce removal, like the story of every successful Indian removal, would have ended with their silent bending to the inevitable. Some friction arose between the settlers and White Bird's Indians, and friction with Indians yielding their homes to superior force is dangerous business — as well strike a match in a powder-mill. There is a story that the white settlers, taking advantage of the Indians' movement of their herds, endeavored to stampede and run off with their horses and cattle,— an act which the exasperated Indians summarily avenged. General Howard says in his report to the War Department: "After examination, it seems to have been a private quarrel, according to Indian story." The version of the Nez Perce agent is probably true, except that the motive is lacking:

"They agreed to move on the reserve by a certain time, had selected the lands upon which to locate, but on the very day that they were to go upon the lands selected — all having left their old or former homes and moved their stock and families to the borders of the reserve — a party of six from White Bird's band commenced the murdering of citizens on Salmon River, thus bringing on another Indian war."

Indians, even Indians grieving over real or fancied wrongs, do not commit indiscriminate murder without some immediate inciting cause; what that was, the official records do not disclose, but the Indians' story of the whites' rapacity remains uncontroverted.

Among Indians in a less inflammable mood, this act of a few vengeful hotheads need not have plunged the whole tribe into war; but the smouldering fire of discontent needed only these murders to turn instantly the whole body of non-treaty Indians from the calm persuasion of their chiefs. By the acts of a few, all were compromised; "the Indians have risen!" went up the cry, and with it ended the peaceful removal so nearly accomplished.

The outbreak occurred many miles east of the Wallowa Valley; neither Joseph nor any member of his band were concerned in it. Yet such was the instantaneous effect of this unhappy incident that to have opposed the common cause of all would have been little short of traitorous; sides were taken in a day, and the non-treaty Indians almost to a man were arrayed with their chiefs against the military.

Then began the Nez Perce war. "The enemy manifests extraordinary boldness," reports General Howard, "planting sharpshooters at available points, making charges on foot and on horseback with all manner of savage demonstrations." After a few preliminary skirmishes, the "war" developed into a pursuit of the Nez Perces — and it was the most remarkable campaign in the annals of Indian warfare. Across into Montana, over the Rocky Mountains, down through the Yellowstone Park, then northward nearly to the British line, Joseph, with his men, women, and children, led General Howard from June until October in a chase of thirteen hundred miles. Joseph fought only when compelled to. In the Bitter Root Valley he traded for goods with the rapacious storekeepers who were traitorous enough to willingly supply his wants. One merchant, however, declined to aid his country's enemies, and closed his store in their faces; the Indians could easily have looted the place, but Joseph was first and last for peace if it could be accorded him. His mode of warfare brought him this tribute in General W. T. Sherman's report to the Secretary of War:

" The Indians throughout displayed a courage and skill that elicited universal praise; they abstained from scalping, let captive women go free, did not commit indiscriminate murder of peaceful families which is usual, and fought with almost scientific skill, using advance and rear guards, skirmish-lines and field-fortifications."

That flight of months before the troops was one long tragedy for Joseph and his people. If it taxed to the utmost the endurance of General Howard's command, what must it have been for the Indians, encumbered with their families? Many fell by the way who were not the victims of their pursuers' bullets; many women and children of Joseph's band were left in hastily made graves. It is a sad truth that desperate men among the fleeing Indians committed a number of robberies and murders which could not be considered as acts of war; but the dishonors of the campaign seem to weigh against General Howard's Indian allies. " See these women's bodies disinterred by our own ferocious Bannock scouts!" writes General Howard. " See how they pierce and dishonor their poor, harmless forms, and carry off their scalps! Our officers sadly look upon the scene, and then, as by a common impulse, deepen their beds, and cover them with earth." (" Joseph Nez Perce.")

Notwithstanding these few barbarities committed on both sides, the campaign was singularly free from incidents that add bitterness to the inevitable horrors of Indian war. Brave and hardy soldiers, doing a stern duty under orders from their Government, pressed to the utmost a band of some six hundred fleeing men, women, and children who could not be made to understand why the country of their fathers from time without reckoning should pass to the white man " by right of discovery and occupation." Many old men in that stricken band had been with Old Joseph when he said, " The land on the other side of the line is what we gave to the Great Father." Is it to be wondered at that the simple Indian mind cried out, " Why has the white man crossed the line? "

The sad story of the American Indian is told in these, " the law of nations " — which does not recognize him, and that other law not made by men or nations, the " Survival of the Fittest " — which dooms him.

United States troops all along the line of flight were called out to intercept the Indians. General Gibbon, making a hasty march from Helena with about two hundred men, came upon Joseph before he had reached the Yellowstone Park, drove him out of his camp with considerable loss, and captured his herd of ponies. Without ponies the Indians' flight would have been of short duration; no one knew that better than Joseph. So, gathering his scattered forces, he turned upon Gibbon, routed him out of the same camp, recaptured his ponies and escaped, leaving eighty-nine Indians dead on the field. Gibbon himself was wounded in the assault.

But fighting with women and children on the field of battle was not to the liking of General Gibbon. " He pointed to where women, during the battle, with their little ones in their arms, had waded into the deep water to avoid the firing; and told me how it touched his heart when two or three extended their babies toward him, and looked as pleasant and wistful as they could for his protection; this was while the balls were whistling through the willows near by." ("Joseph Nez Perce.")

After passing through the Yellowstone Park, and along the borders of the famous Yellowstone Lake, Joseph turned to the northward, with the intention of escaping into the British possessions. By this time troops were being hurried to the scene of action from all parts of the country; even far-off Georgia sent two companies across the continent. In those days, before the United States Government had conceived its mission to impress Christian civilization upon foreign peoples by means of the military, its army was so insignificant that one band of runaway Indians served to draw the whole available force into the field.

Beset with foes in his long journey to the northward across Montana, dodging from one little "army" almost into the clutches of some other, Joseph successfully eluded them all until his escape seemed certain. But finally, in the Bear Paw Mountains, within one day's march of the British line, the Indians were intercepted by a force in command of Col. Nelson A. Miles. There Joseph made his final stand. With all their remaining strength and numbers the Indians desperately fought their last battle. It was a hopeless fight of worn-out men against a superior force of comparatively fresh soldiers. White Bird and a few of his followers escaped through the lines to the British possessions,

The Indian Dispossessed

while Joseph, to save his people from annihilation, surrendered to Colonel Miles, after his brother Ollicut, five other chiefs, and many warriors had been killed in the battle.

"This reply of Joseph's was taken verbatim on the spot," says General Howard's report:

"Tell General Howard I know his heart. What he told me before I have in my heart. I am tired of fighting. Our chiefs are killed. Looking Glass is dead. Too-hul-hul-sote is dead. The old men are all dead. It is the young men who say yes or no. He who led on the young men is dead. It is cold, and we have no blankets. The little children are freezing to death. My people, some of them, have run away to the hills, and have no blankets, no food; no one knows where they are, perhaps freezing to death. I want to have time to look for my children and see how many of them I can find. Maybe I shall find them among the dead. Hear me, my chiefs. I am tired; my heart is sick and sad. From where the sun now stands I will fight no more forever."

Captives at last. A strange tragedy, this, to be enacted on the one hundredth anniversary of the patriots' darkest winter!

1777, 1877; a liberty-loving nation, dwelling at this centennial time on the memories of its own struggle for independence; pointing its youth to the picture of Washington and his men at Valley

The Nez Perces

Forge, — freezing, hungry, and ill-clothed, yet holding out that they might rule their lives as they saw fit; might have dealt generously with a luckless people brought by the same love of liberty to a similar unhappy predicament. But their affliction was only beginning.

It was the intention of their captors to send the Indians back to Idaho. Joseph never ceased to claim that the one condition of his surrender was that he be taken back to Idaho. General Howard states in his report: "I directed Colonel Miles to keep the prisoners till next spring, it being too late to send them to Idaho by direct routes this fall, and too costly by steamer and rail." But no sooner did the good people of Idaho hear of the capture and plans for the return, than they entered a most strenuous protest; Indians once removed would never return if they could prevent it. Once more the "voice of the people" secured the Government's ear and set up the murders by a portion of the tribe as sufficient reason for keeping the Indians forever outside the limits of Idaho. As usual, Washington yielded to the Vociferous Few. The protests of Joseph, the judgment and recommendation of General Howard and Colonel Miles were set aside, and the Indians were ordered to that "graveyard of the northern Indian," the Indian Territory. It was done with a full knowledge of the consequences. The Honorable Commissioner of Indian

Affairs had said in his report to the Honorable Secretary of the Interior, no more than three months before the Nez Perce removal took place:

" Experience has demonstrated the impolicy of sending northern Indians to the Indian Territory. To go no farther back than the date of the Pawnee removal, it will be seen that the effect of a radical change of climate is disastrous, as this tribe alone, in the first two years, lost by death over 800 out of its number of 2376. The Northern Cheyennes have suffered severely, and the Poncas who were recently removed from contact with the unfriendly Sioux, and arrived there in July last, have already lost 36 by death, which, by an ordinary computation, would be the death rate for the entire tribe for a period of four years."

Yet these Nez Perces, accustomed to the high altitude, the cool bracing atmosphere of mountainous Idaho, were to be sent to the hot prairies of the Indian Territory with the full approval of this same Commissioner. The political consideration must have been great to have compelled this fourth sacrifice of human life.

The Indians were first taken to Fort Leavenworth, Kansas, and placed in camp on the Missouri River bottoms for the winter. The change from Idaho to Missouri River bottoms, enough in itself to invite disaster, was aggravated by their surroundings; says an inspector, " Between a lagoon and the river, the

122

worst possible place that could have been selected; and the sanitary condition of the Indians proved it." Here they were kept until well into the following summer: "One-half could be said to be sick, and all were affected by the poisonous malaria of the camp." In the middle of July they were removed to the scorching plains of the Indian Siberia. Here these mountain Indians went down like moths in a flame. Within three months the Commissioner who had recounted the disastrous effects of the climate on the Pawnees, the Cheyennes, and the Poncas made this report:

"After the arrival of Joseph and his band in the Indian Territory, the bad effect of their location at Fort Leavenworth manifested itself in the prostration by sickness at one time of 260 out of the 410, and within a few months they have lost by death more than one quarter of the entire number."

The death rate was so appalling that public attention was attracted; criticisms began to pour in upon the Indian service. Indignant people demanded that something be done, and the Commissioner of Indian Affairs made a personal visit to the tribe:

"Joseph had two causes of dissatisfaction, which he presented to notice in plain, unmistakable terms. He complained that his surrender to General Miles was a conditional surrender, with a distinct promise that he should go back to Idaho in the spring. The other complaint was that the land selected for him on the Quapaw reservation was not fertile, and that water was exceedingly scarce on it; that two wells had been dug to a depth of 60 to 70 feet without reaching water; and that he did not like the country."

Then the Commissioner set out with Joseph and an interpreter in a vain search for some spot in the Territory to Joseph's liking. He continues:

" I travelled with him in Kansas and the Indian Territory for nearly a week and found him to be one of the most gentlemanly and well-behaved Indians that I ever met. He is bright and intelligent, and is anxious for the welfare of his people."

Joseph never lost an opportunity to assert his understanding of the terms of surrender. His agent reports:

" Joseph expresses himself as very much opposed to making this country his future home, dwelling particularly on what he claims were the terms of surrender agreed upon between himself and General Miles at Bear Paw Mountain, according to which he argues he was to be returned to his old home."

This claim of Joseph, so often repeated, receives no official comment in the records. It is given each time simply as a declaration coming from Joseph, unaccompanied by so much as a statement that he is mistaken. To get at the facts, the author appealed for information to the best possible authority — Gen. Nelson A. Miles. With characteristic cour-

tesy the General supplied this clear account of the
surrender:

" WASHINGTON, D. C., June 3, 1904.

" DEAR SIR:

" Your inquiry of 1st received. When
Chief Joseph was surrounded and held for five days
with no possible chance of escape he asked under a
flag of truce what would be done with him in case
he surrendered. He was informed that so far as I
knew it was the intention of the Government to send
him back to the Idaho reservation and require him
to stay there. I do not think there was any other
purpose or design on the part of the authorities at
that time, and I have always believed that that
should have been done.

The sending of Joseph and the Nez Perces to the
Indian Territory, where a large percentage of them
died from malaria, was an after-consideration, and
in my opinion a serious mistake. The location of
his tribe, however, was not a condition of his surrender, for he surrendered, and was compelled to
surrender, by force of arms.

But, in my opinion, the ends of justice would
have been reached had he been returned at once
to his reservation; and justice has been delayed by
his being forced to remain in another part of the
country.

" Yours truly,

" (Signed)   NELSON A. MILES."

The Indian Dispossessed

The Indian language does not contain qualifying clauses; the Indian mind does not comprehend them. It is easy to understand how Joseph could have mistaken the General's reply that, *so far as he knew*, the Indians were to be returned to Idaho.

Popular indignation was pressing hard upon the Commissioner of Indian Affairs; and the righteous wrath of justice-loving citizens has to be reckoned with as well as the importunities of the Vociferous Few.

" The extinction of Joseph's title," he says, " to the lands he held in Idaho will be a matter of great gain to the white settlers in that vicinity, and a reasonable compensation should be made to him for their surrender. It will be borne in mind that Joseph has never made a treaty with the United States, and that he has never surrendered to the Government the lands he claimed to own in Idaho. On that account he should be liberally treated upon his final settlement in the Indian Territory."

Passing strange, this recognition of the Indian title *after*, and not before, the Indian's summary expulsion from his country! Possibly it was compelled by public opinion; and surely, with the Indian country gained, Washington could safely indulge a conscience which at an earlier stage would have been fatal to its plans. The Commissioner continues in the same strain:

" The present unhappy condition of these Indians

appeals to the sympathy of a very large portion of the American people. I had occasion in my last annual report to say that 'Joseph and his followers have shown themselves to be brave men and skilful soldiers, who, with one exception, have observed the rules of civilized warfare, and have not mutilated their dead enemies.' These Indians were encroached upon by white settlers on soil they believed to be their own, and when these encroachments became intolerable they were compelled, in their own estimation, to take up arms. Joseph now says that the greatest want of the Indians is a system of law by which controversies between Indians, and between Indians and white men, can be settled without appealing to physical force. He says that the want of law is the great source of disorder among Indians. They understand the operation of laws, and if there were any statutes the Indians would be perfectly content to place themselves in the hands of a proper tribunal, and would not take the righting of their wrongs into their own hands, or retaliate, as they now do, without the law. In dealing with such people it is the duty, and I think it will be the pleasure, of the department to see that the fostering hand of the Government is extended toward them, and that it gives them not only lands on which to live and implements of agriculture, but also wholesome laws for their government."

The Indian Dispossessed

One cannot read the Indian records of the past fifty years without being impressed by the persistent denial to the reservation Indian of civil law, or of laws necessary to take the place of the tribal control which he was compelled to surrender. Year after year good men in the service filled the record with appeals for adequate Indian law, but every attempt to secure congressional action was effectually blocked by the interested few in Congress.

And why? For no other reason than that the reservation Indian, as one of a herd, without permanency, without organization or legal recourse, lent himself more readily to the successive removals which were compelled by successive demands for the best of his remaining land. Deny this as they may, or seek to excuse it on the ground of the Indian's incompetence, it is to their lasting dishonor that for their own personal gain a people boasting the equality of *all men* should have steadily denied to the Indian the one thing by which he might hope to come into an advantageous relation with the superior race, — recognition under the law. And once more, here is the deadly parallel; in the Declaration of Independence, this is set down as *first* in the arraignment of King George:

" *He has refused his assent to laws, the most wholesome and necessary for the public good.*"

The history of oppressed peoples is much the same in all ages, and among all nations; and this

great nation may well join in Kipling's supplication:

> "Judge of the Nations, spare us yet,
> Lest we forget, lest we forget!"

The story of Joseph's band in the Indian Territory
is told in successive annual reports:

"A day school was opened in February, 1880, and
has been very successfully run under the care of
James Reubens, a full-blood Nez Perce, with an
average daily attendance of twenty.

"The Nez Perces are a religious people, and under
the intelligent teachings of Mr. Reubens they are
strict observers of the Sabbath, refusing to perform
any labor whatever upon that day. Twice upon the
Sabbath they meet together, and listen to the preach-
ing of Mr. Reubens, and sing hymns, with an occasional prayer. Their services are conducted with
as much order and the congregation is as much interested in the proceedings as any body of white
people in any church in the land."

Again, in the following year:

"The Nez Perces, located at Oakland, comprise
three hundred and twenty-eight souls, and I am sorry
to be compelled to report that there has been a large
amount of sickness and many deaths among them
during the last year. This arises from the fact that
they have not become acclimated, and are to a great
extent compelled to live in tepees, the cloth of which

9

The Indian Dispossessed

has become so rotten from long wear and the effects of the weather as to be no longer capable of keeping out the rain, by which they were soaked during the last spring. The tribe, unless something is done for them, will soon become extinct. Of all Indians with whom I have become acquainted, they are by far the most intelligent, truthful, and truly religious. . . .

" Love of country and home, as in all brave people, is very largely developed in this tribe, and they long for the mountains, the valleys, the streams, and the clear springs of water of their old home. . . .

" The number of females outnumbers the males by more than one hundred. This surplus is caused by the widows whose husbands fell during the war. These poor women are all longing to return to Idaho, to their friends and relations. I would suggest the propriety of returning them to their old homes, where they will be more comfortable than they are at present, and, I believe, would not be a greater expense to the department than they are here. So brave, good, and generous a people deserve well of their Government, and I can only express the hope that such generous action will be taken by the coming Congress in their behalf as may enable the department to furnish them with the horses and implements of agriculture that they so much need. Such a people should not be allowed to perish, and this great Government can afford to be generous and just."

The Nez Perces

And the year after:

"Filled with a love of country — almost worshipping the high mountains, bright flashing streams, and rich fertile valleys of Idaho — they have inherited and transmitted to their children a name for bravery, for truthfulness, and honor of which they may indeed be proud. The unfortunate war into which they were driven in 1877 with the United States is far from being a blot on their escutcheon, and all brave, high-minded people the world over will honor them for their gallant defence of their homes, their families, and their hunting-ground. When they surrendered to superior force they did it in the most solemn manner and under the most solemn promises of protection and a return to their own country. That that promise has not been kept is an historical fact, and never has been explained. Might never made right, and the power to punish can never excuse its exercise wrongfully. As the years go by the eyes of this people are turned to the Northwest, and their yearning hearts pulsate naught but Idaho. Like Inspector Pollock, I can exclaim, 'Of all men in the world, is it possible that we *two* only can see this wrong!'"

The Commissioner of Indian Affairs is finally constrained to recommend their return to Idaho:

"The deep-rooted love for the 'old home,' which is so conspicuous among them, and their longing desire to leave the warm, debilitating climate of the

Indian Territory for the more healthy and invigorat-
ing air of the Idaho Mountains, can never be eradi-
cated, and any longer delay, with the hope of a final
contentment on their part with their present situation,
is, in my judgment, futile and unnecessary. In view
of all the facts, I am constrained to believe that the
remnant of this tribe should be returned to Idaho,
if possible, early next spring."

During the following year, by permission of the
Department, " twenty-nine Nez Perces, mostly the
widows and orphans of those killed in the war,"
were returned to the reservation in Idaho, but Congress turned a deaf ear to the plea of the tribe.
Their story continues in the reports:

" These Indians are in some respects superior to
those of any other tribe connected with the agency.
They are unusually bright and intelligent; nearly
one-half of them are consistent members of the
Presbyterian Church. They meet regularly for
weekly services in the school-house, and so far as
dress, deportment, and propriety of conduct are
concerned they could not be distinguished from an
ordinary white congregation. The entire band, with
perhaps one or two exceptions, are quiet, peaceable,
and orderly people. They receive what is provided
for them with apparent thankfulness, ask for nothing more and give no trouble whatever. They are
extremely anxious to return to their own country.
They regard themselves as exiles. The climate does

132

not seem to agree with them, many of them have died, and there is a tinge of melancholy in their bearing and conversation that is truly pathetic. I think they should be sent back, as it seems clear they will never take root and prosper in this locality."

The successive annual enumerations of the Nez Perces might have furnished Congress food for reflection, had it taken the trouble to consult the reports. Four hundred and ten were originally taken to the Indian Territory. Then, while the first great epidemic of disease was taking off one quarter of their number, a considerable remnant of "non-treaty" Nez Perces was captured in Idaho and brought to the Territory, thus swelling the number of survivors to 391. Then follow successively the annual counts: 370, 344, 328, 322, 282 (29 widows returned), 287, and finally, after seven years of life in the Indian Territory, 268. At this rate of decrease the last Nez Perce would have departed for the happy hunting-ground within twenty years.

But philanthropic persons were impressed by this steady reduction of the tribe, if the Indian bureau was not, and in this seventh year nothing less than a thoroughly aroused public opinion, pointedly expressed, compelled the return of these Indians to the Northwest. To the *Northwest*, but not all to their people in Idaho; another element had to be reckoned with, — the stern opposition of the Idaho settlers. The Indian bureau, with no policy except to please, with its ear to the ground, listening to the divided clamor of the people, met this divided sentiment most curiously by *dividing the Indians*, restoring less than half to the Nez Perce reservation, while the others, including Joseph and his more immediate following, were sent to an Indian reservation in northeastern Washington to continue their exile.

All history acquits Joseph and his band in the Wallowa Valley of the murders which decided the " non-treaty " Indians for war. Nevertheless, Joseph had led the combined forces in their hopeless struggle; and afterward it was Joseph's voice that was raised in continual protest against the extinction of his people. So, in the selection of a scapegoat to offer up to the good people of Idaho, the lot naturally fell to Joseph. It was the irony of fate that he who had mainly accomplished the restoration of his people was not to participate in it. And again, the irony of fate that fifteen of White Bird's band — the band concerned in the murders — should at this same time have been received back from their retreat in British territory and given good land in the home reservation of the Nez Perces.

The restoration of the favored portion to their own tribe is reported by the Nez Perce agent:

" One hundred and eighteen Nez Perces of Joseph' band reached this agency June 1, 1885, were kindly received, and have gone out among the tribe. Afte an absence of eight years they return very much broken in spirit. The lesson is a good one and furnishes profitable study for the more restless of the tribe who are not disposed to settle down and enter upon civilized pursuits. They seem inclined to profit by experience. Some have already taken up lands and are fencing the same, while others will follow next spring."

There, as the story goes, "they lived happily ever after."

And from Colville agency in Washington comes this tirade:

"Last June a remnant of Joseph's band was brought from the Indian Territory, numbering 150, and placed upon this reserve — taken from a country where they had already become acclimated, where they had their well-fenced fields, their bands of cattle and horses, their children at school, and in fact progressing finely, rationed by the Government as well, and on account of the sickly sentiment expressed in the East towards them removed to Idaho and Washington Territories, against the wishes of the people of these territories, whose relatives were slain by this band, whose outrages and atrocities will last in the minds of these settlers as long as they have being. It is said that they have been removed back to this country by the Government at their own request, and that in a great measure they will be expected to care for themselves on account of lack of sufficient appropriations. What can they do for the next year until they can harvest a crop? Joseph says: ' We have nothing. My people cannot and will not starve, and if we are not fed we will go and find it.' Why was this not thought of before they came here? My estimates for food for them were cut down and they were placed on short rations until they appealed to the military, and have since been fed. I earnestly recommend that Congress provide sufficiently for their wants early in the session."

This reflects the sentiment of the gentle settler. What are the facts of history to him!

With this final disposition of Joseph's band the Indian spirit seems to have been broken. Departing hope left behind a listless indifference. Indian agents came, and Indian agents went, each wondering at their settled inaction. This report, after five years, is much like those from the Indian Territory:

" *Joseph's band of Nez Perces* are more or less unsettled and of a restless character; they appear to be greatly dissatisfied at times with their location. In my opinion the causes of their dissatisfaction are just. Owing to many of their friends and relatives living on the Nez Perce reservation in the State of Idaho, an effort should be made to remove them from their present location at Nespilem to the Nez Perce Agency, Idaho, where they claim land would be allotted to them, as is being done with their friends and relatives of that reservation. I have taken particular notice of the fact that when they receive letters from their relatives living on the Nez Perce reservation or a visit from their friends from that reservation they appear to have the 'blues' and at once express a strong desire to return to their old home. I am thoroughly satisfied they will never be content to remain on this reservation, no matter how well they may be treated by the Government."

Did ever the Government heed an Indian appeal for the sake of the Indians alone? Public clamor had been stilled by Joseph's removal to *the North-west*, and far-off Nespilem best suited the Government as the final location for Joseph's band.

The Indian comprehends civilization only as it comes within range of his vision. He takes it as he sees it. What had Joseph seen in the white man's civilization? In his earlier years, the many broken promises of the Government; white encroachment and aggression; the strong hand of the military; the violation of what he held to be a sacred promise, then seven years of slow death; and now, another land of exile, with the heritage from Old Joseph, the Wallowa Valley, forever lost to his people. Why should Joseph meekly bend to a system which had made of his tribe an unhappy people? What was there worth striving for in a civilization so full of injustice toward his race?

Back, back to the Indian way, said Joseph; back

The Indian Dispossessed

to the tepee, and to the blanket; back to the Indian
traditions, and to the simple Indian notion of justice; back to the Indian life in search of lost happiness! The story of the American Indian reservation
contains many a tale of Indian retrogression, but
none more marked than that of Joseph's band. Every
reservation can show its quota of old-time Indians
carried over from the old Indian life into the semi-
captivity of the present day, — unprogressive always,
frowning their impotent protest as they recall the
happier hunting days, — not a grand, but a sad army
of old warriors who failed to win in the fight for
liberty and country.

And so the older Indians in Joseph's band idly
dream of the good old days in the Wallowa, while
the young men go uncontrolled; there are none of the
activities and incentives of the real Indian life; there
are all of the white man's vices to fill their place.

Fifteen years of this life pass, and Joseph feels
old age coming upon him. Then he dreams an
impossible dream. It is that he shall take his people
back to the Wallowa Valley — that he may die in
the land of his fathers.

Did ever an exiled Indian more blindly reckon without the white possessors of his old hunting-ground?
No Indian petition to his Great Father in Washington
could prevail against such a report as this:

"The subject of Joseph's transfer to the Wallowa
Valley in Oregon has been discussed at length among

138

them during the year and has had a demoralizing effect upon them. . . . A liberal Government has treated him with a generosity scarcely having a parallel, and his entire lack of appreciation is clearly shown in his unblushing audacity in asking for more liberal assistance in being transferred to another territory."

"Asking for more"! Here we have another Oliver Twist. The agent continues:

"It is true that the Wallowa Valley is the birthplace of Joseph and that there lie the bones of his forefathers, and he no doubt entertains many kind and pleasant remembrances of his younger life. Boyhood with its sweet memories furnishes food for deep reflection, and he no doubt cherishes the thought of some day returning, but in my opinion by his actions in after years he has forfeited all his rights and privileges to enjoy the blessings of a peaceful and happy life in his old home. . . . His reason for a transfer from his present home is purely sentimental, bolstered up by a personal ambition. . . .

"It is true Joseph fought with much gallantry, but when finally overcome he was tendered the generous hand of a beneficent Government. In my opinion any act, its ultimate object being the removal of Joseph and his followers to either Idaho or Oregon, would be an injudicious one. The horrors of long ago lie at his threshold and are pleading for justice. The appalling wrongs done by him

The Indian Dispossessed

are crying from the blood-stained soil of Idaho for restitution. Joseph's life would be jeopardized should he ever return for a permanent residence in a territory he previously occupied."

Then the Commissioner of Indian Affairs takes it up:

"Last March Chief Joseph visited this city and submitted to this office a petition to be allowed to leave his present location on the Colville reservation in Washington and return with his band of about 150 Nez Perces to Wallowa Valley, Oregon. This, he claimed, was the home of his ancestors and was his own home until he and his people were removed from Idaho to the Indian Territory in 1877, at the close of the Nez Perce war. By Department reference the office also received a communication, dated April 7, 1900, from Maj. Gen. Nelson A. Miles, United States Army, recommending that Joseph's request be granted."

But there are a hundred objections, according to the Commissioner. The Wallowa Valley contains four prosperous towns; Wallowa Lake "is fast becoming a favorite summer resort"; the land is worth " from $20 to $75 per acre "; and, mark ye well, the Wallowa Valley contains 1,017 precious votes! This asset is set forth with great particularity in a table arranged by precincts. " It would be very expensive to secure any portion of Wallowa Valley upon which to locate those Indians." He concludes:

140

The Nez Perces

" While a majority of the settlers of the Wallowa Valley retain no ill will against the Nez Perces for the troubles of 1877, yet there are some whose relatives were ravished and killed by Indians on Salmon River and Camas Prairie during that outbreak who vow vengeance against all members of the band, and more particularly against Joseph, and many of the settlers predict that should the Indians be returned to this valley to stay permanently Joseph would be assassinated within a year."

Here again is the threat of assassination for crimes that he never committed. During all these years Joseph had lived in perfect safety within easy reach of the bereaved settlers, but were he to " ever return for a permanent residence " or, " to stay permanently," in other words, *to occupy some of their precious land*, then their gentle grief would rise to the pitch of murder. What finely balanced sorrow this, to be so weighed in the commercial scale!

It was an impracticable, impossible thing, this dream of a homesick Indian. So Joseph returned to his people. Four years more of idle longing; then, in September, 1904, Joseph departed for the happy hunting-ground, where treaties are not made to be broken, and liberty is real.

" The line was made as I wanted it; not for me, but my children that will follow me; there is where I live, and there is where I want to leave my body.

The Indian Dispossessed

The land on the other side of the line is what we gave to the Great Father."

Wise and far-seeing old chieftain, to save a country for his people! Poor Indian, poor fool, to think that his " Great Father " would turn back the faithful who might cross the line set down in the covenant!

THE REMOVAL OF THE PONCAS

"I see you all here to-day. What have I done? I am brought here, but what have I done? I don't know. It seems as though I have n't a place in the world, no place to go, and no home to go to." *Chief Standing Bear.*

SPREAD out the map of the state of South Dakota; begin at the southeastern corner, and follow up the Missouri River to the mouth of the Niobrara; then up the river again, only a finger's breadth, to Ponca Creek. If the map is one of the present day, the name of Ponca will attach only to the creek, for that flows on forever; if it is a map of fifteen years ago, a small strip of land between Ponca Creek and the Niobrara River may bear the name " Ponca Indian Reservation." If so, it is only because the name clings to the country that had belonged to the Ponca Indians a dozen years before.

But twenty-eight years ago, and one hundred years ago, and how much longer ago nobody knows, for the white man's history of that region dates no farther back, the Ponca Indians dwelt in this fertile country of wooded valleys and upland prairies, a little band distinct from all the Indians around. During all those years they maintained their country

143

against the repeated incursions of the powerful Sioux on the north with a vigor and tenacity born of the Indian love of the land of his fathers.

The tide of white occupation that flowed to the Northwest during the early fifties was temporarily checked by the Sioux on the upper Mississippi, who at that time ruled supreme in the greater part of Minnesota and all of Dakota, and it then took the course of least resistance, — through Iowa, and into eastern Nebraska. This placed the Poncas between the hostile Sioux on the north and the white settlements on the south, — a situation well calculated, in the ordinary course of events, to hasten the day when Ponca Creek should become the monument of the tribe. But this circumstance really gave the Poncas a new lease of life. They met the advancing whites with the hand of friendship, while the high-strung Sioux (with the exception of the Yancton and one or two other small tribes of the Sioux nation) resisted the invasion with a ferocity that dismayed even the reckless frontiersmen. The keen settlers were quick to perceive the strategic value of a friendly tribe between themselves and the powerful hostiles:

" I cannot speak in too high terms of the uniform good conduct of this tribe. While many other Indians have been fighting the Government, and murdering the frontier settlers, this tribe and the Yancton Sioux have remained faithful to their

WHITE EAGLE, HEAD CHIEF OF THE PONCAS
(1877)

treaty stipulations, and stood as a barrier between the hostile Indian and the white settler upon the frontier."

So, under shelter of this gentle band, the white man rested for a time while he gathered strength for the next advance; and just so long as the Poncas were of service " as a barrier between the hostile Indian and the white settler," they were treated with a consideration rarely accorded to an Indian people so insignificant in numbers, so unassertive, and possessed of so good a country.

But in course of time the inevitable demand for more of the Indian country made itself felt in Washington. In 1858 a treaty was entered into with the Poncas, by the terms of which they ceded much of their territory for certain considerations. Article I. recites the cession of territory and defines the tract that is guaranteed to them. Then follows:

" Article II. In consideration of the foregoing cession and relinquishment, the United States agree and stipulate as follows, viz.:

" First. To protect the Poncas in the possession of the tract of land reserved for their future homes, and their persons and property thereon, during good behavior on their part."

The second stipulation secured to the Poncas the payment of annuities extending over a period of twenty-five years. Other benefits, such as schools, agency, etc., were provided for. The Poncas appear to have been fairly satisfied with the treaty, except that their ancient burial-ground was not included in the portion left to them. This situation was remedied by a supplementary treaty in 1865, in which the bounds of their reservation were moved eastward a few miles, but still between, and at the confluence of, the Missouri and Niobrara Rivers, where the tribe had been discovered sixty odd years before. The provisions of the treaty of 1858 were in nowise altered or disturbed. The record shows what generous treatment will do for an Indian tribe:

" The ratification of the supplementary treaty with the tribe has greatly encouraged them. It not only gives to them their old burying-grounds, but gives them a tract of land in every respect much better for agricultural purposes than their former location. . . .

" In agricultural pursuits the members of this tribe are becoming quite proficient. They have between 500 and 600 acres of corn and other vegetables, which have all been well cultivated, and now bid fair to yield a very heavy harvest."

The superintendent reports in 1866:

" PONCAS. Since my acquaintance with this tribe, for a period of upwards of five years, they have remained faithful to their treaty obligations in every particular, under circumstances at times that would have palliated, if not excused, a hostile attitude on their part. The unprovoked and fiendish attack made by a party of drunken United States soldiers in the fall of 1863 upon a small number of this tribe, while making their way to their reservation and home from a friendly visit to a neighboring tribe, the Omahas, by which seven of them lost their lives and considerable property, would have been considered, in a civilized community, as a sufficient cause for retaliating upon their murderers or their relatives, especially if no effort was made to indemnify the sufferers, by the Government who had permitted its soldiers to perpetrate such wrongs."

Among the murdered were three women, a little girl, and an infant. Their supplementary treaty provided for the payment of damages to the relatives of the deceased.

Not many Indian tribes have had praise so heaped upon them. In 1869 their number is given as 768. The agent reports:

"The Ponca Indians are in no way addicted to drinking or gambling, neither will they spend their money for whisky. They fully understand the use of money, and will use it to the very best possible advantage. I am fully of the opinion that if their annuity were paid to them in money, they would use it more judiciously for their comfort than it could possibly be used for them in the purchase of goods. The Poncas are the most peaceable and law-abiding of any of the tribes of Indians. They are warm friends of the whites, and truly loyal to the Government, and they fully deserve its consideration and protection."

And again:

" I respectfully submit the following report of the Ponca school. The school was opened May 1, 1871, and has continued to the present date, with an average attendance of 17 girls and 33 boys. The children have been taught in the common English branches, and have made a good degree of progress, learning quite as readily as white children. The parents and relations of the scholars exhibit great interest in the advancement of their children, and to their influence is to be attributed the regular attendance."

The next year three schools are reported, with an average attendance of seventy-seven.

In their earnest striving after the white man's way, the Poncas were constantly beset by the horde of hostile Indians on their unprotected border. The records mention these raids at different times, and in 1873 the untamed Sioux seem to have been more than usually active:

" But far worse is the record of disasters from frequent engagements with hostile Indians, who come in force to fight in disproportionate numbers these poor, ill-armed, but really brave Indians, peaceably imbibing and receiving the practical lessons of civilization, and proving to their friends their evident desire to better their condition. . . .

The Removal of the Poncas

" The Poncas, having thus almost unaided kept the enemy at bay with little better than clubs and bows and arrows, and fought their way through a season of greater peril from hostile Indians than has ever before been encountered by them, as I am informed, ask only that guns of long range and capacity for speedy execution be put into their hands; and this application I would earnestly indorse and urge upon the attention of the Department as an act of justice to these brave men, who are struggling upward to the light, and if protected in their persons and property, and given such efficient aid as their rate of progress requires, will, as the evidences bear me out in saying, make a record that cannot but justify the benevolent intentions of the Government, and prove beyond cavil that the Indian can be and will be made to contribute to the general welfare, and can appreciate while he shares the benefits and blessings he has with others earned. . . .

" We have a few plain signals with the bell and the voice, which all well understand, and which evoke always a ready response. There are no cowards in camp, except it be the young women and small children; the old women, when they are not permitted to fight, urge on the lagging and make most excellent camp followers."

Notwithstanding the solemn treaty pledge " To protect the Poncas in the possession of the tract of land reserved for their future homes, and their persons and property thereon," this band of hapless Indian farmers still served well as a buffer between the hostile Indian and the white settler. At this time the "peace policy" — or, rather, its "inverted" substitute — was in full force; and under the acknowledged interpretation of it, "that the expenditures of the Government should be proportioned not to the good but to the ill desert of the several tribes," the Government was purchasing an uncertain immunity from attack from these same hostiles by the liberal distribution of rations, while they followed their murderous pastimes in the Ponca country. But the attacks of the Sioux became much less frequent during the next two years, and with eighty children in school, a church of two hundred members, and one hundred and fifty comfortable houses, the Poncas were much like any white community of peaceful farmers. Then in 1876 came this cheering news from the agency of the Lower Brule Sioux, — the half-wild Indians who had so long harassed the Poncas:

"During the year the chiefs and head-men of the tribe asked for and obtained permission to visit the Ponca agency, for the purpose of making a treaty with the Poncas, with whom they have been on unfriendly terms for years. This treaty was effected and entered into in the best of faith."

With this only serious difficulty so satisfactorily

adjusted, there was no apparent reason why these Indian farmers should not make rapid advance along the " white man's road."

No *apparent* reason. But events of far-reaching importance had meanwhile been transpiring in the great Sioux Country north of them, — events of such importance that a tribe so insignificant as the Ponca, had it only known, might well have trembled for its future at the hands of a Government whose avowed policy was to bestow its favors on the powerful and hostile Indians in the interest of peace.

Away to the Northwest stretched the great Sioux reservation, from the Missouri River on the east to the western line of Dakota. The territory embraced was as large as the State of New York, and fifty thousand Sioux drew rations from the various Government agencies upon it. The appropriations for these Indians were about two million dollars annually, — an amount ridiculously in excess of treaty stipulations, but no more than sufficient to prevent serious hostilities. In the extreme western part of this great reservation lay the Black Hills, with their millions of treasure still uncovered. Explorations made in the early seventies disclosed the presence of gold; in 1874 a military expedition was sent into the Hills to explore the country, and in the following year a commission endeavored to obtain from the Indians a cession of that portion of their country — but the attempt ended in failure.

The Indian Dispossessed

But the cry of gold had gone up, and the white man's progress was not to be stayed by an Indian refusal. The horde of gold-seekers came up from the Union Pacific railroad and the overland wagon routes on the south, as far as the southern line of the Sioux reservation. And there they stopped. Directly in this natural gateway to the Black Hills were some fourteen thousand Sioux, under Spotted Tail, the most diplomatic Indian politician of his time, and Red Cloud, an acknowledged leader in the great Sioux nation.

"No passing through," said they; "until another bargain is made with the Great Father, this is Indian country." Then the cry of the Vociferous Few went up to Washington, — the old, old cry for Indian removal, — and again the Government heard "the voice of the people."

The Black Hills must be cleared of Indians; so must the gateway on the south. But how propitiate the untamed Sioux?

The Indian ring sought eagerly for some especially favored spot for the powerful chiefs, Spotted Tail and Red Cloud; something to serve up to them as a token of kindly regard.

There, at the southeast corner of the great reserve, was the land of the Poncas, — a prize for any Indian chief. And why not? One hundred and fifty houses, five hundred acres of growing crops, — just the place to teach the astute Spotted Tail, or Red

RED CLOUD, OGALALLA SIOUX CHIEF

(1876)

The Removal of the Poncas

Cloud, the warrior, the gentle arts of the white man.

The Poncas? Some eight hundred of them — what were they compared to the recovery of the Black Hills? The treaty? Hang the treaty!

And the public? What cared the Vociferous Few, so long as the great American people slept on under the delusion that they were really " the people "?

The records show a most careful development of the scheme. During the years 1875 and 1876 there appeared four executive orders, adding to the Sioux reservation on the north a considerable area, and on the east — along the east bank of the Missouri River — a country as large as the state of Massachusetts. These immense additions on the east foreshadowed the removal of the Black Hills section of the Sioux tribes eastward to the Missouri River.

The Commissioner of Indian Affairs, in his report for 1875 to the Secretary of the Interior, suggests the removal of the Poncas to the Omaha reserve, in eastern Nebraska, ending with the naïve remark that " The country where they now are would make a suitable location to which the Red Cloud Sioux could be removed. It is hoped that provision may be made by the next Congress for such removal."

All details having been perfected, the necessary legislation for the whole scheme was secured at one stroke. On August 15, 1876, an appropriation for the Sioux Indians was made by act of Congress, with certain provisions; among them:

"Hereafter there shall be no appropriation made for the subsistence of said Indians, unless they shall first agree to relinquish all right and claim to any country outside the boundaries of the permanent reservation established by the treaty of eighteen hundred and sixty-eight for said Indians; and also so much of their said permanent reservation as lies west of the one hundred and third meridian of longitude."

The first clause is aimed at their hunting privilege outside their permanent reservation, as provided for in their treaty of 1868; the second cuts off from the west side of their reservation a country as large as the State of Connecticut, *including the Black Hills.*

Another stipulation:

"And unless they will receive all such supplies herein provided for, and provided for by said treaty of eighteen hundred and sixty-eight, at such points and places on their said reservation, and in the vicinity of the Missouri River, as the President may designate."

This relates to the eastward movement of the Black Hills Sioux.

And lastly:

"*Provided further,* That the Secretary of the Interior may use of the foregoing amounts the sum of twenty-five thousand dollars for the removal of the Poncas to the Indian Territory, and providing them a home therein, with the consent of said band."

This is the first mention of the Indian Territory in connection with the Poncas. The only hope of these farmer Indians now lies in the provision for their consent. The worst that the Commissioner had hinted at as being in store for the Poncas was removal to the Omaha reservation, — in eastern Nebraska, not a great distance from their own. The Omahas were intermarried extensively with the Poncas, and a removal to that reservation would have entailed no extraordinary hardship.

But the *Indian Territory!* The graveyard of the northern Indian condemned to spend his days in exile there!

The Commissioner of Indian Affairs, commenting in 1874 on removals to that country, says:

" It has heretofore been considered feasible eventually to domicile a large majority of the Indians in this Territory. Experience, however, shows that no effort is more unsuccessful with an Indian than that which proposes to remove him from the place of his birth and the graves of his fathers. Though a barren plain without wood or water, he will not voluntarily exchange it for any prairie or woodland, however inviting."

But in this year, 1876, what does the Commissioner say?

155

" Steps are being taken for the removal of the Poncas from their present location in the south-eastern corner of Dakota to the Indian Territory. Their exposure to raids from the Sioux, whose hostility arises from the fact that the Poncas are on lands claimed originally by the Sioux and included in their permanent reservation, has hitherto been a serious obstacle in the way of the progress in civilized life which they seem disposed to make. It is believed that when the necessity of giving a large share of attention to self-defence is removed they will readily come into a condition of self-support by agriculture."

The Commissioner expressed this tender solicitude for the welfare of the Poncas under date of October 30; he had the report of his agent, dated August 11, setting forth their treaty of peace with the Sioux. With that report before him, why was he attempting to accomplish their removal to avoid a condition which had already ceased to exist? His next sentence reveals the cause of his sudden interest in their welfare:

" The proposed removal will not only benefit the Poncas, but the reserve thus vacated will offer a suitable home for some of the wild bands of Sioux, where, with a set of agency-buildings, one hundred Indian houses, and five hundred acres of improved land to start with, the experiment of their civilization may be tried to advantage.

The Removal of the Poncas

"For this removal, conditioned on the consent of the Poncas, Congress at its last session appropriated $25,000. If the efforts now being made to gain such consent are successful, the move will be commenced in early spring."

This provision for the consent of the Poncas proved to have been a most indiscreet concession on the part of Congress. The efforts to gain the Indian consent were continued well into the winter, and in January an inspector took ten of the chiefs to the Indian Territory to show them the country.

There are two entirely different tales of this trip to the South. Here is the story as discreetly told by the Honorable Commissioner of Indian Affairs:

"Unfortunately, the delegation of ten chiefs, on account of the failure of the Osages to show hospitality, inclement weather, and other causes, became disheartened at the outset, declined the friendly advances of the Kaws, refused to look farther, scarcely noticed the rich lands along the Arkansas River, and on reaching Arkansas City, eight left in the night on foot for the Ponca agency, which they reached in forty days."

The Indians relate a dark tale of attempted coercion, with the alternative of being cast adrift, without money, interpreter, or guide, in a strange land four hundred and fifty miles from home, if they refused to select a location for their tribe and agree to removal. According to the story of one of the eight chiefs, they replied that "it would be better for ten of us to die than that the whole tribe, all the women and little children, should be brought there to die, and die we all would, right there, rather than do what they asked."

The remaining two chiefs were induced to make a selection of land, and chose a location on the Quapaw reservation in the Indian Territory. Then the inspector returned, and continued his efforts to gain the consent of the Poncas. What he gained is told in the report of their newly appointed agent for 1877:

"In obedience to instructions received from the Indian Office, I left Hillsdale, Michigan, on the 24th day of April last, arriving at Columbus, Nebraska, on the 28th, at which place I had expected to find Agent Lawrence with the Ponca tribe of Indians en route for their new home in the Indian Terri- tory. In this I was disappointed, as Lawrence ar- rived on the same day with only 170 of the tribe; more than three-fourths of the tribe having refused to leave their old reservation in Dakota, stating, as reported to me, that they preferred to remain and die on their native heath, in defence of their homes, and what they claimed to be their rights in the land composing the reservation upon which they were living, than to leave there and die by disease in the unhealthy miasmatic country which they claimed had been selected for them in the Indian Territory."

The Removal of the Poncas

This was the result of the winter's work, — one hundred and seventy out of a total of seven hundred and thirty Indians. How had Washington taken their refusal to move?

On March third, attached to an appropriation bill providing for the removal of the Black Hills Sioux to the Missouri River, Congress passed a *second* act for the removal of the Poncas:

"*And provided further*, That the sum of fifteen thousand dollars of this appropriation, in addition to that heretofore appropriated, may be used for the removal and permanent location of the Poncas in the Indian Territory."

It will be perceived that this act bears a striking resemblance to the one of August 15 preceding, which has already been quoted, except that the words "with the consent of said band" are omitted. The inference is that the resourceful Uncle Sam, finding himself handicapped by this provision in the first act, decided to simply legislate the matter of Indian consent out of existence. This inference may be considered as far-fetched; indeed, it may be asserted that it is monstrous to impute a motive so atrocious to the mere omission of one phrase.

Let the public records express the Government's intent. In a later report, containing executive orders and other papers relating to Indian affairs, is this statement:

"*Ponca Reserve.* By the Indian appropriation act

of August 15, 1876 (19 Stats., p. 192), an appropriation was made for the removal of the Poncas
to the Indian Territory when they should consent
to go. By the Indian appropriation act of March 3,
1877 (19 Stats., p. 287), an additional appropriation
was made for the same purpose, but there was nothing contained therein respecting their consent. Under
these acts the Poncas were removed to the Quapaw
reserve."

And again, more clearly, in the official " Schedule
of Indian Land Cessions" are found these two entries:

" 1876. Aug. 15, Act of Congress. Stat. L.,
XIX, 192 — Ponka — Provides for removal of
Poncas to Indian Territory whenever they consent.
See Acts of Congress for March 3, 1877, . . ."

" 1877. March 3, Act of Congress. Ponka —
Provides for their removal to Indian Territory
without regard to their consent. They were removed under this act and temporarily located in
the Country of the Quapaw, . . ."

There is a grim, though possibly unintentional,
humor in recording under the title of " Indian
Land Cessions" the removal of a tribe of Indians
from their native heath " without regard to their
consent." A further perusal of this remarkable
book suggests a change of title in the interests of
candor.

But the Indian consent was no longer to be reckoned with in carrying out the grand scheme for

160

the recovery of the Black Hills. By this clever device the attitude of the Poncas in withholding their consent to give up their land became at once one of opposition to the Government. To gain their consent, when their consent was a legal requirement, was one thing; to overcome the unwillingness of these Indian farmers to obey an act of Congress was quite another.

The Honorable Commissioner of Indian Affairs continues his recital to the Honorable Secretary of the Interior:

"It having been determined that the removal of the remainder of the tribe must now be insisted upon, troops were ordered to the Ponca agency. But it was decided to forestall the need of their presence by sending back the Ponca agent, Mr. Lawrence, with his successor, Agent Howard, to again urge upon the Indians a quiet compliance with the wishes of the Government. They so far succeeded as to be able to request that the four companies who had started for the agency be recalled, and on the 16th of May the last Ponca crossed the Niobrara and turned his face southward."

This is the manner of the agent's success:

"On the 15th, I held another council, which was largely attended by the chiefs, head-men, and soldiers of the tribe, and which was of more than four hours' duration. At this council the Indians maintained that the Government had no right to move

The Indian Dispossessed

them from the reservation, and demanded as an inducement or equivalent for them to give up the reservation and move to the Indian Territory, first, the payment to them by the Government of the sum of $3,000,000; and, second, that before starting, I should show to them the sum of $40,000, which they had been told had been appropriated by the Government for their removal. To all of which I replied positively in the negative, telling them that I would not accede to nor consider any demands that they might make, but that I would take under my consideration reasonable requests that they might submit touching their removal, and, as their agent, do what I could for them in promoting their welfare; that I demanded that they should at all times listen to my words; that they should go with me to their new home, and that they should, without delay, give me their final answer whether they would go peaceably or by force. The Indians refused to give answer at this time, and the council closed without definite results, and the Indians dispersed with a sullen look and determined expression.

"On the following morning, however, May 16, they sent word to me at an early hour that they had considered my words and had concluded to go with me, and that they wanted assistance in getting the old and infirm, together with their property, over the Niobrara River, which was much swollen by the rains and at a low temperature. I at once employed

162

from the young men of the tribe a suitable number for the purpose, and at five o'clock P. M. had the entire tribe with their effects across the river, off the reservation, and in camp in Nebraska."

Twenty-five soldiers had been in service at the Ponca agency while the " consent " of the one hundred and seventy was being secured; they seem to have furnished the necessary showing of force. Confronted with the choice of going either " peaceably or by force," these unarmed people naturally concluded to go peaceably. The soldiers escorted them for the first twelve of their fifty-two days' journey south, to insure their going.

This total disregard of the protests of the Indians, and their removal with a display of force, has been dwelt upon at great length by all writers of Ponca history, under the impression that the action was in direct violation of the provision in the removal act, to first gain their consent. The legislation designed to remedy this annoying feature of the first act seems to have wholly escaped notice. It should be conceded that while the national pledge, humanity, justice, and Christian dealing were put aside, the provision for the Indian consent was not violated; it was legislated out of existence. The Indians were removed under the *second* act of Congress.

But in the blaze of indignation which swept over the country when the main facts of the Ponca removal became known, every official in Washington connected with the affair rested meekly under the charge of violation of the consent clause. Not once do we find this *second* act of Congress set up to stem the tide of popular reproach. It may be considered that, in this, good judgment assisted their discretion.

Then comes the story of the journey southward, — and these are extracts from the " Journal of the March," as it is designated in the records:

" *May* 21. Broke camp at seven o'clock, and marched to Crayton, a distance of thirteen miles. Roads very heavy. The child that died yesterday was here buried by the Indians, they preferring to bury it than to having it buried by the white people.

" *May* 23. The morning opened with light rain, but at eight o'clock a terrific thunder-storm occurred of two hours' duration, which was followed by steady rain throughout the day, in consequence of which we remained in camp. During the day a child died, and several women and children were reported sick, and medical attendance and medicine were obtained for them.

" *May* 24. Buried the child that died yesterday in the cemetery at Neligh, giving it a Christian burial.

" *May* 27. The morning opened cold, with a misty rain. Rain ceased at half-past seven o'clock, and we broke camp at eight, and marched eight miles

The Removal of the Poncas

farther down Shell Creek, when, a heavy thunderstorm coming on, we again went into camp. Several of the Indians were here found to be quite sick, and, having no physician and none being attainable, they gave us much anxiety and no little trouble. The daughter of Standing Bear, one of the chiefs, was very low of consumption, and moving her with any degree of comfort was almost impossible, and the same trouble existed in transporting all the sick.

"*May 29.* Major Walker, who had accompanied us from the Niobrara to this place with twenty-five soldiers under orders from the War Department, took leave of us and returned to Dakota.

"*June* 3. Had some trouble in getting started. Broke camp at eleven o'clock, and marched eight miles. Went into camp on Blue River. Many people sick, one of whom was reported in a dying condition. Had bad roads, and rained during the afternoon.

"*June* 5. Broke camp at seven o'clock. Marched fourteen miles, and went into camp near Milford. Daughter of Standing Bear, Ponca chief, died at two o'clock, of consumption.

"*June* 6. Remained in camp all day for the purpose of obtaining supplies. Prairie Flower, wife of Shines White, and daughter of Standing Bear, who died yesterday, was here given Christian burial, her remains being deposited in the cemetery at Milford, Neb., a small village on Blue River.

The Indian Dispossessed

"In this connection I wish to take official knowledge and recognition of the noble action performed by the ladies of Milford in preparing and decorating the body of the deceased Indian woman for burial in a style becoming the highest civilization. In this act of Christian kindness they did more to ameliorate the grief of the husband and father than they could have done by adopting the usual course of this untutored people, and presenting to each a dozen ponies.

"*June* 8. Broke camp at Milford, and marched seven miles. Roads very bad. Child died during the day.

"*June* 9. Put the child that died yesterday in the coffin, and sent it back to Milford to be buried in the same grave with its aunt, Prairie Flower.

"*June* 14. Water-bound, and had to remain in camp all day waiting for creek to run down. The Otoe Indians came out to see the Poncas, and gave them ten ponies.

"*June* 16. Broke camp at seven o'clock, and reached Marysville, Kans., where we went into camp. During the march a wagon tipped over, injuring a woman quite severely. Indians out of rations and feeling hostile.

"*June* 18. Broke camp at seven o'clock. Marched nine miles, and went into camp at Elm Creek. Little Cottonwood died. Four families determined to return to Dakota. I was obliged to ride nine miles on horseback to overtake them, to restore harmony, and settle difficulty in camp. Had coffin made for dead Indian, which was brought to camp at twelve o'clock at night from Blue Rapids. A fearful thunder-storm during the night, flooding the camp equipage.

"*June* 19. The storm of last night left the roads in an impassable condition, and in consequence was obliged to remain in camp all day. Buried Little Cottonwood in a cemetery about five miles from camp.

"*June* 25. Broke camp at six o'clock. Marched to a point about fifteen miles farther up Deep Creek. Two old women died during the day.

"*June* 26. The two old women who died yesterday were given Christian burial this morning.

"*June* 30. Broke camp at six o'clock. Passed through Hartford, and camped about six miles above Burlington. A child of Buffalo Chief died during the day.

"*July* 1. Broke camp at six o'clock. Marched twelve miles, and went into camp. Purchased a coffin at Burlington, and gave the dead child of Buffalo Chief a Christian burial at that place."

Christian burial seems to have been the only good thing the agent had to offer these exiles. He continued the good work, for six weeks later he says, "Since the arrival here there have been eight deaths, all of which have been given Christian burial with but small expense to the service."

Far out upon the bleak steppes of northern Asia,

where the Russian exiles slowly drag themselves to *their* Siberia, are the old and infirm, the little children and consumptive girls, who give up the weary struggle and sink by the wayside, accorded the inestimable boon of Christian burial? The heart sickens at the thought that they are not. A copy of this " Journal of the March " should be presented to the Czar, that he may learn with what exquisite tenderness a more enlightened Government attends the last rites of its victims.

Further perusal of this agent's very complete report gives us a picture of the situation and outlook:

" I am of the opinion that the removal of the Poncas from the northern climate of Dakota to the southern climate of the Indian Territory, at the season of the year it was done, will prove a mistake, and that a great mortality will surely follow among the people when they shall have been here for a time and become poisoned with the malaria of the climate. Already the effects of the climate may be seen upon them in the *ennui* that seems to have settled upon each, and in the large number now sick.

" It is a matter of astonishment to me that the Government should have ordered the removal of the Ponca Indians from Dakota to the Indian Territory without having first made some provision for their settlement and comfort. Before their removal was carried into effect an appropriation should have been made by Congress sufficient to have located them in their new home, by building a comfortable house for the occupancy of every family of the tribe. As the case now is, no appropriation has been made by Congress, except a sum of but little more than sufficient to remove them; no houses have been built for their use, and the result is that these people have been placed on an uncultivated reservation to live in their tents as best they may, and await further legislative action.

" The rainy season, which I am informed usually commences in this country from the 1st to the 15th of September, will soon be upon them, and before any appropriation can be made by Congress for the construction of houses, winter will have set in, and they will be obliged to remain in their tents until spring, which will be but a poor protection for their families against the elements."

The agent's gloomy predictions, based on the climatic conditions and the lack of shelter, were duly verified. The official record of deaths for the ensuing year was eighty-five; the Indians mourned the loss of one hundred and fifty-seven; but if there is any virtue to be extracted from the fact that one-seventh, instead of one-fifth, of the entire tribe was sacrificed within the first year, the Indian service is welcome to it.

The agent next proceeds to lecture his Government on the question of title:

" As the matter now stands, the title to this reservation remains in the Quapaws, no effort having been made as yet to even remove them from it; and the title to the old Ponca reservation in Dakota still remains in the Poncas, they having signed no papers relinquishing their title nor having violated any of the provisions of the treaty by which it was ceded to them by the Government.

" These Indians claim that the Government has no right to move them from their reservation without first obtaining from them by purchase or treaty the title which they had acquired from the Government, and for which they rendered a valuable consideration. They claim that the date of the settlement of their tribe upon the land composing their old reservation is prehistoric; that they were all born there, and that their ancestors from generations back beyond their knowledge were born and lived upon its soil, and that they finally acquired a complete and perfect title from the Government by treaty made with the ' Great Father ' at Washington, which, they claimed, made it as legitimately theirs as is the home of the white man acquired by gift or purchase. They now ask that a delegation of their chiefs and head-men be allowed to visit Washington for the purpose of settling all matters of difference between them and the Government; and that they may talk to the ' Great Father ' face to face about the great wrongs which they claim have been done them.

" I earnestly recommend that their request be granted."

The Removal of the Poncas

It may be interesting to learn which of the Black Hills Chiefs succeeded to the ancient home of the Poncas, — Red Cloud or Spotted Tail? Two months later the Honorable Commissioner of Indian Affairs, with this full Ponca record before him, reported to the Honorable Secretary of the Interior the selection of a location for Red Cloud farther up the Missouri. Then he says:

" For the latter [Spotted Tail], the old Ponca reserve was decided upon, where the agency dwellings, store-houses, one hundred and fifty Indian houses, and five hundred acres of cultivated fields, left vacant by the Poncas, offer special advantages for present quarters."

And with the Sioux it is the same old story of the Indian attachment to the soil. In his next sentence the Commissioner complains that " the Spotted Tail and Red Cloud Indians persisted in making strenuous objection to such removal," — but they were removed, and Spotted Tail soon dwelt, an exile, in the home of the Poncas.

What is home? Four walls? A palace? It may be high mountains and a green valley; rocks and a stream; or a sea of brown grass waving in the wind. It is the one spot in nature that entwines our earliest thoughts, which ripen with maturing years into tender memories. And those who dwell nearest nature know best the ties of home.

The Indian Dispossessed

In considering the Indians' appeal to Washington, the Commissioner says, in the same report:

" A delegation of the tribe recently visited Washington and presented to the President their earnest request to be allowed to return to their old reservation in Dakota or to join the Omahas, a kindred tribe, in Nebraska. The obvious unwisdom and even impossibility of removing Indians *from* the Indian Territory necessitated a refusal of their request; but they were given permission to select a permanent home upon any unoccupied lands in the territory which the Government still owns. They were urged to take immediate steps to effect a settlement of the matter, and were promised, as soon as the locality should be decided upon and Congress should provide the necessary funds, such assistance in the way of schools, houses, stock, seeds, tools, agricultural implements, etc., as would enable them to more than replace the property and improvements unwillingly relinquished in Dakota; but they were made distinctly to understand that all assistance by the Government would be in the line of teaching them self-helpfulness, and would be conditioned on exertions put forth by themselves in that direction."

The italics are those of the Commissioner. It is difficult to discover any process of reasoning in the words " obvious unwisdom and even impossibility," but that italicised word " *from* " furnishes the key to the settled policy of removals to the country which the Indians have always regarded as "the graveyard of the Indian race." Indians may go *to,* but never *from* that country. Originally intended as an exclusive refuge for the American Indian, where he might learn the ways of civilization and eventually become a part of the national life as an Indian State, the Indian Territory had degenerated into a general dumping-ground for every tribe that in its own home was an obstruction to the grand scheme of national upbuilding. The only removals *from* the Indian Territory were those of the grim reaper, and his harvest among the outcasts seems to have been viewed with settled complacency.

These are some of the expressions of the Commissioner before the storm of popular disfavor broke upon Washington. Now observe the change. One year later, stung by the most severe criticism, beset on all sides by lovers of justice, this same Commissioner extends his tender sympathy:

" In this removal, I am sorry to be compelled to say, the Poncas were wronged, and restitution should be made as far as it is in the power of the Government to do so. For the violation of their treaty no adequate return has yet been made. They gave up lands, houses, and agricultural implements. The houses and implements will be returned to them; their lands should be immediately paid for, and the title to their present location should be made secure. But the removal inflicted a far greater injury upon

the Poncas, for which no reparation can be made,
— the loss by death of many of their number, caused
by change of climate."

Again this curious recognition of the Indian title
after, and not before, the Indian has been dispossessed — but without a suggestion of restoring the
land.

How changed is the tone of official Washington
when above the clamor of the Vociferous Few rises the
real, the unmistakable " voice of the people "; of a
high-minded people, outraged, burning with shame
that the Government of " all the people " should lend
itself to the intrigues of a handful of mountebanks!

A year after their removal to the Indian Territory,
the Poncas, *again* removed one hundred and eighty-
five miles farther west, were still living in tents;
their agent says:

" Their sufferings have greatly discouraged and
made them dissatisfied with this location, and they
express a strong desire to go back to their old
reservation in Dakota. However, I am of the opinion that if the Government will fully and promptly
fulfil all the promises made to them to induce them
to leave Dakota and take up their home on this
reservation they will cheerfully accept the situation
and settle down with a determination to labor and
better their condition. At present there is a restless, discontented feeling pervading the whole tribe.
They seem to have lost faith in the promises of the

Government, and often say the 'Great Father' has forgotten them; by the time he again remembers them none will be left to receive what he has promised them. The chiefs are very anxious to visit Washington and have a talk with the President for the purpose of having the size and boundaries of their reservation determined and definitely settled by treaty stipulations. I would earnestly recommend that they be allowed to do so some time during the coming winter. I think it would contribute greatly toward a restoration of good feeling, and to remove the spirit of discontent and dissatisfaction which now pervades their minds.

" The Poncas are good Indians. In mental endowment, moral character, physical strength, and cleanliness of person they are superior to any tribe I have ever met. I beg for them the prompt and generous consideration of the Government, whose fast and warm friends they have ever been."

This appeal of the Indians for a second talk with with their " Great Father " in Washington was not granted. Denied the recognition of their treaty right to their old home, and discouraged in the hope of ultimate justice, the Poncas, homesick, heartsick, sick in body, began to escape from their reservation in small parties, in the hope that they might make their way back to die in the land of their fathers. The story of the wanderings of these little bands five hundred miles through a strange

The Indian Dispossessed

country to their beloved Dakota home is most pathetic; that any of them reached the North alive is wholly due to the quick sympathy and assistance of benevolent people through whose country they passed, and of many others who had learned of their affliction. A few of these Poncas reached their old neighbors, the Santees, whose reservation was a few miles east of the old Ponca home. The Santee agent reports:

"During the last year about thirty Poncas came among us asking that they could be allowed to stay, stating they had been taken to a very hot place and many of their friends had died, and they were heart-sick and wished the Santees to have pity on them and allow them to stay up here in this good land among them. The councillors consented, and they are among us sending their children to school and making a good start."

Another little band, in the early spring of 1879, set their faces northward under the guidance of Chief Standing Bear. It will be remembered that the daughter of Standing Bear, Prairie Flower, died on the march to the South; many of his relatives and all but one of his children died in the Indian Territory. The last to die was his oldest son, a young man who could speak and read English, the hope and dependence of his aged father. The dying boy, according to the later testimony of Standing Bear, begged his father to take his body back to

CHIEF STANDING BEAR
(1877)

the old home for burial, and the broken-hearted chief, hoping at the same time to save the lives of his wife and only remaining child, placed the bones of his boy in an old trunk, and with fifty of his followers escaped from the reservation. After enduring incredible hardships, thirty of them reached their kindred tribe, the Omahas, who dissuaded them from at once attempting to continue on their journey to the old Ponca reserve, for they were sick and without provisions and the necessary implements to establish homes for themselves. The Omahas induced Standing Bear to remain with them, gave his party land, tools and seed to plant it, and those of the Indians who were not too ill to do so went to work.

But the Interior Department did not propose to have any Ponca bands within a possible marching distance of their old home. Under orders of the War Department troops were sent to the Omaha reservation to take the party South. They came upon these Indians, half of them still sick, the others ploughing and planting, acquainted them with the orders of the Department, and once again the Poncas took up the weary march, back to their Siberia, still bearing the trunk containing the bones of Standing Bear's son.

They were first taken to Fort Omaha, situated on the outskirts of the city of Omaha. In an incredibly short time their story was being told about the city; a day or two later, one Sunday, several churches passed resolutions after their regular services, and the pastors joined in a telegram of protest to the Secretary of the Interior. Friends of the Indian race in Washington were at once informed, and appealed in person to both the Secretary of the Interior and the Commissioner of Indian Affairs.

All this availed nothing; the final word from Washington ordered their return to the Indian Territory. But this set-back served only to stimulate the good people of Omaha in their efforts. Attorneys were then interested in the case, and on a writ of *habeas corpus* the whole question of the detention and removal of Standing Bear's band was brought into the United States District Court for Nebraska for a hearing, on the ground that the Indians had committed no crime and were deprived of their liberty without due process of law.

The Interior Department strenuously opposed this measure of relief. The counsel for the Government, in an argument of several hours' duration, maintained that Standing Bear was not entitled to the protection of a writ of *habeas corpus*, on the ground that an Indian was not a *person* under the law, and had no standing in the courts; while the equally able attorneys for the Indians contended that such protection was intended to apply to *every human being*, and that any other interpretation of the law

178

The Removal of the Poncas

was in violation of the fundamental principles of the Constitution.

This is a bit of Standing Bear's testimony:

"*A.* He says, when I got down there, I saw the land, and the land was not good to my eye; some places it looked good, but you kick up the soil a little, and you found lots of stones. It was not fit to farm. When we got down there we heard we were going to get clothing, and get money, and everything that we wanted, but I have not seen it yet. When I was told to go down there, I thought, perhaps, the land was good, and I could make a living, but when I got down there it was entirely different from the land in my own home. I couldn't plough, I couldn't sow any wheat, and we all got sick, and couldn't do anything. It seemed as though I had no strength in my body at all. The hot climate didn't agree with me. But when I came back here I seemed to get strength every day. Instead of our tribe becoming prosperous, they died off every day during the time. From the time I went down there until I left, one hundred and fifty-eight of us died. I thought to myself, God wants me to live, and I think if I come back to my old reservation He will let me live. I got back as far as the Omahas, and they brought me down here. I see you all here to-day. What have I done? I am brought here, but what have I done? I don't know. It seems as though I haven't a place in the world, no place to

go, and no home to go to, but when I see your faces
here, I think some of you are trying to help me, so
that I can get a place sometime to live in, and when
it comes my time to die, to die peacefully and happy.
(This was spoken in a loud voice, and with much
emphasis.)

"*The Court.* Tell the witness to keep cool."

The opinion of Judge Dundy begins with these
words:

"During the fifteen years in which I have been
engaged in administering the laws of my country,
I have never been called upon to hear or decide a
case that appealed so strongly to my sympathy as
the one now under consideration. On the one side
we have a few of the remnants of a once numerous
and powerful, but now weak, insignificant, unlettered, and generally despised race. On the other, we
have the representative of one of the most powerful, most enlightened, and most Christianized nations of modern times. On the one side we have
the representatives of this wasted race coming into
this national tribunal of ours asking for justice and
liberty to enable them to adopt our boasted civilization and to pursue the arts of peace, which have
made us great and happy as a nation. On the
other side we have this magnificent, if not magnanimous, Government, resisting this application with
the determination of sending these people back
to the country which is to them less desirable

than perpetual imprisonment in their own native land."

It may seem beyond belief that in the one hundred and third year of the declaration, "all men are created equal," it was necessary for a federal judge to determine at great length that every human being is a *person*, and as such entitled to a hearing in the courts, but pages of the decision are given to this phase of the case; even the dictionary is appealed to. The Judge says:

"Webster describes a 'person' as 'a living soul; a self-conscious being; a moral agent; especially a living human being; a man, woman, or child; an individual of the human race.' This is comprehensive enough, it would seem, to include even an Indian."

The Judge reviews the circumstances at the time of the arrest, and at considerable length leads up to his decision:

"To accomplish what would seem to be a desirable and laudable purpose, all who were able so to do went to work to earn a living. The Omaha Indians, who speak the same language, and with whom many of the Poncas have long since continued to intermarry, gave them employment and ground to cultivate so as to make them self-sustaining. And it was when at the Omaha reservation, and when *thus* employed, that they were arrested by order of the Government for the purpose of being taken back to the Indian Territory. They claim to be unable to see the justice, or reason, or wisdom, or *necessity* of removing them by force from their own native plains and blood relations to a far-off country in which they can see little but new-made graves opening for their reception. The land from which they fled in fear has no attractions for them. The love of home and native land was strong enough in the minds of these people to induce them to brave every peril to return and live and die where they had been reared. The bones of the dead son of Standing Bear were not to repose in the land they hoped to be leaving forever, but were carefully preserved and protected, and formed a part of what was to them a melancholy procession homeward. Such instances of parental affection, and such love of home and native land may be *heathen* in origin, but it seems to me that they are not unlike *Christian* in principle. . . .

"I have searched in vain for the semblance of any authority justifying the commissioner in attempting to remove by force any Indians, whether belonging to a tribe or not, to any place, or for any other purpose than what has been stated. Certainly, without some specific authority found in an act of Congress, or in a treaty with the Ponca tribe of Indians, he could not lawfully force the relators back to the Indian Territory, to remain and die in that country, against their will. . . . If they could be removed to the Indian Territory by force, and kept there in the same way, I can see no good reason why they might not be taken and kept by force in the penitentiary at Lincoln, or Leavenworth, or Jefferson City, or any other place which the commander of the forces might, in his judgment, see proper to designate. I cannot think that any such arbitrary authority exists in this country.

" The reasoning advanced in support of my views leads me to conclude:

" First. That an *Indian* is a PERSON within the meaning of the laws of the United States, and has therefore the right to sue out a writ of *habeas corpus* in a federal court, or before a federal judge, in all cases where he may be confined, or in custody under color of authority of the United States, or where he is restrained of liberty in violation of the Constitution or laws of the United States.

" Second. That General George Crook, the respondent, being the commander of the military department of the Platte, has the custody of the relators under color of authority of the United States, and in violation of the laws thereof.

" Third. That no rightful authority exists for removing by force any of the relators to the Indian Territory, as the respondent has been directed to do.

" Fourth. That the Indians possess the inherent right of expatriation as well as the more fortunate white race, and have the inalienable right to ' *life,* *liberty,* and the pursuit of happiness,' so long as they obey the laws and do not trespass on forbidden ground. And —

" Fifth. Being restrained of liberty under color of authority of the United States, and in violation of the laws thereof, the relators must be discharged from custody, and it is so ordered."

Liberty! Bereft of homes and goods, mourning their many dead, yet Liberty came to these benighted Indians as a ray of light in the darkness. Standing Bear, taking from his few treasures a war-bonnet, a tomahawk, and a pair of buckskin leggings, sought out his three greatest benefactors — the gentleman who had first discovered his distress, and the two attorneys who conducted his case without expectation of reward — and presented to them the simple tokens of his gratitude:

" A little while ago I had a house and land and stock. Now I have nothing. It may be that some time you may have trouble. You might lose your house. If you ever want a home come to me or my tribe. You shall never want as long as we have anything. All the tribe in the Indian Territory will soon know what you have done. While there is one Ponca alive you will never be without a friend." [1]

But freedom did not bring with it the restoration of a single right to their goods and lands. They

[1] "The Ponca Chiefs."

were destitute, and without a home. The members of the Omaha Committee, with substantial aid from many other friends of the Indian, succeeded in gathering about one hundred of the refugee Poncas near their old reservation. The number was soon increased to one hundred and seventy-five. The Santee agent's report for the ensuing year takes notice of them:

"In my report last year I spoke of a number of Ponca Indians who had come among the Santees. Since then they have nearly all left, and they are now living on an island, about three miles above Niobrara, adjoining their old reservation. I visited them a short time ago and found they numbered 103 souls. They have considerable corn; are making hay and building houses for the winter. They have been and are now receiving some assistance from an organization at Omaha which has been created for their relief."

Consternation was upon the autocrats of the Indian Ring. An Indian a *person?* Impossible. Entitled to the protection of the courts? A dangerous proposition. The Indian would be lost to the Inner Circle as a political asset if freedom were extended to him. The case was promptly appealed, but, in the language of the records:

"At the May term, 1879, Mr. Justice MILLER refused to hear an appeal prosecuted by the United States, because the Indians who had petitioned for the writ of *habeas corpus* were not present, having been released by the order of DUNDY, J., and no security for their appearance having been taken."

It would have required something more than a cordial invitation to bring Standing Bear again into the clutches of his Great Father.

Much more that is interesting in the Ponca case does not appear in the official reports. The case of Standing Bear brought the public to its highest pitch of indignation over the Ponca outrage. Public meetings were held in condemnation of the whole affair, and attention was called to many other instances of the Government's perfidy in its dealings with its helpless wards. In Boston a committee was appointed, with Gov. John D. Long of Massachusetts as chairman, to investigate the wrongs of the Poncas; money was raised to determine in the courts the legality of holding the remaining members of the tribe in the Indian Territory, and to restore their old home to them. The Secretary of the Interior was appealed to by persons of prominence in both official and civil life to sanction such a test of the matter in the courts. Again, all this availed nothing. The official argument is of much the same satisfying and convincing order as " The obvious unwisdom and even impossibility of removing Indians *from* the Indian Territory."

The most miserable of all the official excuses put forward was based upon an incomprehensible blunder of the Government. It will be remembered that in 1858 the Poncas had their home guaranteed to them by solemn treaty. In 1868 a treaty was entered into with the Sioux, and, in loosely defining the bounds of their reservation as the Missouri River on the east and Nebraska on the south, the entire Ponca reservation, lying just *north* of the Nebraska line, was unwittingly included in that allotted to the Sioux. Now nothing is clearer than that this mistake should have been at once rectified by obtaining from the Sioux a relinquishment of the Ponca tract; a Government that could peremptorily demand of the Sioux the cession of the entire Black Hills on pain of starvation could have obtained this small concession by even less strenuous methods. It is equally clear that the vested rights of the Poncas could not equitably be disturbed in this settlement, which was a matter only between the Government and the Sioux.

That such a blunder could have been made, and allowed to stand for eight years, shows with considerable clearness the Government's disregard for the integrity of its Indian treaties; it is still more significant that, after eight years, this " unfortunate blunder " made its official appearance coincident with the plan to remove the Spotted Tail and Red Cloud Sioux to the Missouri; but the saddest service of this miserable excuse was to block the way to the restoration of the Ponca homes. Time and again the chroniclers in the public records admit the wretched business, and as many times deny restitution. The Commissioner of Indian Affairs says:

" By a blunder in making the Sioux Treaty of 1868, the 96,000 acres belonging to the Poncas were ceded to the Sioux. The negotiators had no right whatever to make the cession. . . ."

Here is one of the most ludicrous defences in the records:

" By a treaty made by the Government with the Sioux in 1868, the Ponca lands were ceded to them by mistake, so that both tribes claimed the land; the Poncas had the oldest and best title, but the Sioux being so much stronger, and regarding and treating the Poncas as trespassers, were fast sending them to the ' happy hunting-grounds,' and thus the question presented itself to the Government, the duty of protecting the weak against the strong, of saving human lives; this was paramount to the question of title, because, conceding as it did the Ponca title to be good, *the Government was unable to protect them* in the peaceable enjoyment of it, and the only just and humane thing it could do was to move them out of the reach of their oppressors. The Government could pay for the spoliation, but it could not restore the dead to life."

This is really too silly to deserve comment. In all the pilfering Sioux raids, not a dozen Poncas were actually killed; yet one hundred and fifty-seven were sent to the "happy hunting-grounds" by the removal within one year.

The Honorable Carl Schurz, as Secretary of the Interior, and nominally at the head of Indian affairs, had visited upon his undeserving head the odium of the whole Ponca business. His open letters to Governor Long, Senator Dawes, and Mrs. Helen Jackson (the author of " Ramona " and " A Century of Dishonor ") are laden with his tale of personal woe. They reveal an able advocate with a pitifully weak case, but he valiantly makes the best of it. Here are a few fragments from a letter to Governor Long:

" The old Ponca reserve in southeastern Dakota, a tract of 96,000 acres, was confirmed to that tribe by various treaties. In 1868 a treaty was concluded with the Sioux by which a reservation was granted to them, including the tract which formerly had by treaty been confirmed to the Poncas. The Sioux treaty of 1868 was ratified in the usual way and became the law of the land. The Poncas, however, continued to occupy the ceded tract."

So the Sioux treaty became the law of the land. What became of the Ponca treaty? This raises a question: If the Government confirms a tract of land to one tribe, then unwittingly deeds it to another tribe, which gets the land? Justice might point to the first tribe. The Government, with the power to deliver to either, seems to have taken its choice.

The Secretary's personal defence is the only convincing feature in the correspondence. He shows clearly that the whole scheme involving the Ponca removal was laid by the preceding administration, although consummated immediately after he took office. Of this he says:

"The removal itself, in pursuance of the law quoted, was effected a very short time after I took charge of my present position, when, I will frankly admit, I was still compelled to give my whole attention to the formidable task of acquainting myself with the vast and complicated machinery of the Interior Department. If at some future day you, Governor, should be made Secretary of the Interior, you will find what that means; and although you may accomplish it in a shorter time than I did, yet you will have to pass through some strange experiences during the first six months."

In view of the subsequent career of the distinguished Governor, this friendly warning is rather interesting. But there is a depth of meaning in the secretary's admission. When revolting tales come from the realm of the Czar of remorseless cruelties, of stifled justice, and hopeless exile, the world is now enough enlightened to say, "'T is not the Czar — look to the bureaucracy." So, in the land of the Noble Free; secretaries may come to grope their uncertain way, and secretaries may go with the passing of the presidents, but the bureaucracy sits tight at the public crib, guiding unseen the affairs of state. " 'T is not the Czar — look to the bureaucracy."

But as an apologist Secretary Schurz lapses into the mediocre. Of that terrible winter for the Poncas, when an inquisition of months wrung " consent " from one hundred and seventy of them, he says:

" As to the measures taken by Mr. Kemble to obtain what he represented as the consent of the Poncas to the relinquishment of their lands and their removal to the Indian Territory, it may be said that he followed a course which unfortunately had been frequently taken before him on many occasions. Having been a man of military training, he may have been rather inclined to summary methods; moreover, it is probable that as the Ponca reserve had been ceded to the Sioux by the treaty of 1868, and as Congress had provided also that the Sioux should be removed to the Missouri River, and the Sioux were the same year to occupy that part of the country, the removal of the Poncas may have appeared to Mr. Kemble a necessity, in order to prevent a collision between them and the Sioux which would have been highly detrimental to both."

As it was the pre-arranged intention to remove the Black Hills Sioux *directly into the Ponca houses*, an inspector even less astute than Mr. Kemble might have perceived the " necessity " of getting the Poncas out of the way. It was his business to *gain*, not ask for, the Indian consent.

The Indian Dispossessed

The question of the Poncas' fundamental right to their old homes is buried under a mass of argument against their restoration on the ground of inexpediency, none of which is convincing. The terrible Sioux bogey appears again; but Spotted Tail dwelt as unwillingly in the homes of the Poncas as the Poncas remained in the South. He remained there a few months; then, long before the Poncas had ceased to beg for their return, Spotted Tail peremptorily ordered his Great Father to take his people back to *their* old home, on pain of another Sioux war. Within ten days the wily old chief's camp was on wheels, merrily rolling toward the Rosebud country. Spotted Tail, gentle reader, was a Big Chief in the Sioux nation.

Here is a miserable excuse of the Secretary for a great nation to lean upon:

" But another difficulty arose of a grave nature: the invasion of the Indian Territory by white intruders striving to obtain possession of certain lands in the Indian Territory held for Indian settlement in that region, of which the present Ponca reservation forms a part. . . . The lands coveted by the invaders are held against the intrusion on the ground that they are reserved for Indian settlement. It is important, therefore, that the Indian settlements actually on such lands should remain there at least while the Indian Territory is in danger. To take away the existing Indian settlements from those lands under such circumstances would very much weaken the position of the Government defending them, and encourage the invasion."

To preserve the public domain from *invasion* by a few lawless frontiersmen, — a melancholy service for a handful of half-dead Indians who had once "stood as a barrier between the hostile Indian and the white settler upon the frontier"!

And here is another:

"If the Poncas were now taken from those lands and returned to Dakota, this very fact would undoubtedly make other northern Indians, who have been taken to the Indian Territory, restless to follow their example, such as the Northern Cheyennes [fully fifty per cent dead — one hundred and fifty killed by soldiers while escaping to the North], the Nez Perces [thirty per cent dead], and possibly even the Pawnees [over eight hundred dead out of 2376]. Unscrupulous white men, agents of the invaders, would be quickly on hand to foment this tendency."

The Secretary judged the temper of these three tribes with "deadly" accuracy. They really might have been fired with a desire to get out of the Indian Territory.

Did ever a desperately weak case seek strength from equally desperate argument?

This extraordinary letter called forth a prompt reply from the Boston Committee, signed by John D. Long, chairman. Without a trace of personal feeling, and granting the sincerity of the Secretary in his views, it is a scathing arraignment of the whole miserable business. One characteristic passage will suffice:

"First. Did you commit a cruel and unlawful outrage upon the Ponca Indians in robbing them of their homes? To which you have already answered, *Yes*. Second. Have you lifted a finger for all these three years, during which you say you have so sincerely repented your error, to restore them to their homes? To which you have already answered, *No*. Third. Will you not, even at this last moment, for the sake of the credit of the administration and the country, ascertain, by men in whom the Poncas have confidence, whether those who are still in the Indian Territory do not really wish — having full knowledge that the way is cordially open to them — to rejoin the hundred or more who have escaped and returned to Dakota? And if they do, will you not ask for an appropriation, and do what you can to restore them, also? Can you not apprehend the one fundamental thing, that this land in Dakota is theirs, *theirs*, THEIRS? We beg you to apply to their case, not the wrench of a 'policy,' but for once the good old golden rule — not always bad, even, as a policy — of ' doing unto others as ye would that men should do to you.' It may leave the constitutional ' Indian Policy ' blotted by a drop of the milk of human kindness, but it will leave you a record in the administration of President Hayes upon which you will have no more sincere congratulations than our own."

194

The Removal of the Poncas

Secretary Schurz may have admitted the " cruel and unlawful outrage," but he distinctly proved that he was *not* primarily responsible for it. His argument leaves no question of the sincerity of his opinion that, after this lapse of three years, the happiness and welfare of the Poncas could best be served by establishing them fairly and permanently upon their new reservation. To his mind, expediency was the question of the hour. The original sin was upon the preceding administration and had become immutable law. That was his reason why, for three years, these helpless Indians were left to die, were hounded if they escaped, were refused their piteous request to *again* visit their Great Father, *after* the Spotted Tail Sioux had left the old Ponca home absolutely vacant. The Government had blunderingly given the Ponca lands to the Sioux, and laws, however devilish, had given legal color to the Ponca removal before he came into office. He might " apprehend the one fundamental thing, that this land in Dakota is theirs, *theirs,* THEIRS," and only wring his hands in impotent distress over conditions beyond his control.

The splendid record of Mr. Schurz as a friend of the oppressed forces the conclusion that he really could not undo a villainy when once fastened upon the Department. Then, what unseen force comes out from the iniquitous depths of the Indian bureau to turn the will and tie the hands of such a Secretary of the Interior? Does the underworld supply "the voice of the people," even while the people protest? There is more of concern in this than the mere welfare of a luckless race.

The Ponca agitation finally resulted in an underground scheme to settle the questions at issue and end the contest. It is a tale of chicanery worthy of the Indian bureau. Observe the sequence of dates.

On October 25, 1880, twenty Ponca chiefs and head-men in the Indian Territory affixed their marks to this statement, and their agent forwarded it to the Commissioner of Indian Affairs:

"We, the undersigned, chiefs and head-men of the Ponca tribe of Indians, realize the importance of settling *all* our business with the Government. Our young men are unsettled and hard to control while they think we have a right to our land in Dakota, and our tribe will not be finally settled until we have a title to our present reservation and we have relinquished all right to our Dakota land. And we earnestly request that the chiefs of the Ponca tribe of Indians be permitted to visit Washington the coming winter for the purpose of signing away our right to all land in Dakota and to obtain a title to our present reservation; and we also wish to settle our Sioux troubles at the same time. We make the above request, as we desire to have the young men of our tribe become settled and commence to work on their respective claims.

The Removal of the Poncas

"We also desire to make this visit in order to convince the Government that it is our intention of remaining where we are, and requesting the aid of the Government in obtaining teams, wagons, harness, tools, etc., with which to work our land."

Now read any Indian speech, letter, or other utterance; compare with the phrasing of this; study the desires herein expressed in the light of the Ponca record; then, if it appears reasonable to do so, believe that the Indians dictated this petition, or knew what they were signing.

The next move was calculated to throw dust into the eyes of a critical public. While a delegation of Ponca chiefs was being piloted to Washington to sign away their Dakota reservation, the President announced the appointment of a commission:

"EXECUTIVE MANSION,
"WASHINGTON, D. C., December 18, 1880.

"I request the following gentlemen to proceed to the Indian Territory as soon as may be, and, after conference with the Ponca tribe of Indians, to ascertain the facts in regard to their recent removal and present condition, so far as is necessary to determine the question what justice and humanity require should be done by the Government of the United States, and report their conclusions and recommendations in the premises: Brig.-Gen. George Crook, U. S. A.; Brig.-Gen. Nelson A. Miles,

U. S. A.; William Stickney, Washington, D. C.; Walter Allen, Newton, Mass.

" It is the purpose of the foregoing request to authorize the commission to take whatever steps may, in their judgment, be necessary to enable them to accomplish the purpose set forth.

" General Crook is authorized to take with him two aides-de-camp to do clerical work.

" R. B. HAYES."

The champions of the Ponca cause then rested on their guns; the battle seemed half won.

On December 28, ten days later, before the special commissioners could reasonably have reached the Indian Territory on their mission " to determine the question what justice and humanity require should be done by the Government of the United States," the Ponca chiefs in Washington were induced to sign away all their right and title to the old home on the Missouri.

Four weeks later — on January 25, 1881 — the special Commission reported to the President, setting forth the wrongs and scattered condition of the Poncas — some being on the old Dakota reserve — and recommended:

" That an allotment of 160 acres of land be made to each man, woman, and child of the Ponca tribe of Indians, said lands to be selected by them on their old reservation in Dakota, or on the land now oc-

WHITE SWAN, PONCA CHIEF

(1877)

cupied by the Ponca Indians in the Indian Territory, within one year from the passage of an act of Congress granting such tracts of land. That until the expiration of this period free communication be permitted between the two branches of the tribe."

This is followed by a recommendation of generous appropriations to the Poncas *pro rata* in whichever reserve they choose to locate, and that the question of title to the Ponca land be at once settled. Finally, for the special purpose of re-establishing the Poncas in their old home on the Missouri:

"That the further sum of not less than $5,000 be appropriated for the construction of comfortable dwellings, and not more than $5,000 for the erection of a school-house for the Poncas in Nebraska and Dakota, and that suitable persons be employed by the Government for their instruction in religious, educational, and industrial development, and to superintend, care for, and protect all their interests. We respectfully suggest that the welfare of these Indians requires us to emphasize the necessity of prompt action in settling their affairs, to the end that this long pending controversy may be determined according to the dictates of humanity and justice."

On March 3, by act of Congress, provision was *ostensibly* made for carrying out the various recommendations of the Commission:

"For the purpose of enabling the Secretary of the Interior to indemnify the Ponca tribe of Indians for losses sustained by them in consequence of their removal to the Indian Territory, to secure to them lands in severalty *on either the old or new reservation,* in accordance with their wishes, and to settle all matters of difference with these Indians, one hundred and sixty-five thousand dollars, to be immediately available and to be expended under the direction of the Secretary of the Interior, as follows," etc.

Then the public clamor was stilled. Justice had — in words — been done. But against this seeming intent of the Government to give the Poncas free choice to locate on either their old or new reservation, there is the disturbing knowledge that the Honorable Commissioner had, weeks before, secured a deed of relinquishment from the Poncas in the Indian Territory to their old reservation. Now, what provision was made, in the settlement of the Sioux treaty blunder, for the return of Poncas still in the Indian Territory?

On August 20, of the same year, an agreement was entered into with the Sioux:

" The said tribes of Sioux Indians do hereby cede and relinquish to the United States so much of that portion of the present Sioux reservation as was formerly occupied by the Ponca tribe of Indians, set forth and described by the supplemental treaty between the United States of America and the Ponca tribe of Indians concluded March 10, 1865 (14 Stats.,

675), as may be necessary for the settlement of *that portion of the Ponca tribe under Standing Bear now on or residing near the old Ponca reservation,* for their use and occupation, in the proportion and to the extent of as many tracts of 640 acres each as there are heads of families and male members now of the age of twenty-one years and upwards and unmarried."

No provision whatever was made for any Ponca Indians except those " under Standing Bear now on or residing near the old Ponca reservation." Nowhere is there a line to indicate that the act of Congress providing for their return was ever communicated to the Poncas. The official count two years later shows a net gain of twelve in the Indian Territory, while the Poncas on the old reserve barely hold their own. Not one Ponca was returned to the Missouri. The numbers remain in about the same proportion to this day. The Ponca country was cleared of Indians, with the exception of Standing Bear's band, and in a few years was opened to settlement.

This is the story of the Ponca removal, with inevitable sidelights on the Poncas' guardian. Whom do the facts concern more — the Poncas or the guardian?

THE MISSION INDIANS

" This class of Indians seems forcibly to illustrate the truth that no man has a place or a fair chance to exist under the Government of the United States who has not a part in it." *Hon. Commissioner of Indian Affairs, 1874.*

SOME half-dozen years before the birth of American Independence the Franciscan monks founded, under the protection of the Spanish Government, the first of the famous Indian Missions in what is now Southern California. These worldly-wise missionaries gradually extended their establishments northward, and in the memorable year 1776 they attained their northernmost point in the building of the Dolores Mission near the present city of San Francisco.

The sites of these old missions indicate clearly that while the Franciscans may have had first in mind the spiritual welfare of the native peoples, they were also adepts in the art of husbandry and in the selection of locations for the practice of it. Their system of Indian control points as well to a division of their thought between the welfare of their child-like charges and their own material prosperity. It is certain that under the direction of the Fathers many thousands of the Indians became Christians, learned

202

The Mission Indians

the arts, and adopted the ways of civilization to an extent which raised them greatly above their nomadic kinsmen of the North. They lived in houses on the mission lands, which were at least considered as their permanent homes and descended along family lines much as in more highly organized communities. It is also certain that the carefully trained labor of the Indians was utilized by the shrewd monks to add a wealth of highly cultivated lands, produce, cattle, and sheep to their various missions. The title to the land seems to have generally, if not always, rested in the Fathers, while the valuable accumulation of chattels was held in a more or less modified communism, with the property rights greatly in favor of the Franciscans.

For fifty years the Franciscan missions flourished under the protection of Spain in a manner befitting an institution of such marked benefit to both the Indians and their instructors. If the labor were not altogether one of self-sacrifice, nothing less than a goodly endowment of religious zeal could have held these educated men in utter isolation among an unlettered, inferior people. As we look back upon the work of these men and view the stability of the old mission edifices which still stand in the most fertile spots in Southern California, justice, more than charity, compels the clear recognition of their devotion to the cause of Christianity as *first*, and above all else, with a material prosperity as incidental, — a prosperity justified, deserved, and shared liberally with their Indian wards. The frequent aspersions cast upon the motives of these first pioneers are largely due to the frivolous habit of begrudging all missionaries everything more than the barest means of existence, as though constant attendance upon want and hardship were a portion of their mission.

But with the independence of Mexico in 1822 came the undoing of the Franciscan missions. The Spanish governmental favor under which they had prospered for a half-century was lost to them; the Mexican attitude became one of distinct hostility. If this were to be a story of Mexican misrule it would call for more than the mere statement that within fifteen years the last of the Franciscan missions ceased as an organization of the Franciscan monks, but for our purpose the bare recital of fact suffices.

With the passing of the Franciscans the mission lands were in many cases allotted in parcels to the Indians living on them; in other instances no record appears of any Indian title beyond the possessory title which comes from generations of occupancy. Although deprived of much needed protection, the Mission Indians continued to live on and cultivate their lands, while a few remaining zealous adherents of the faith kept them together and attended their spiritual and temporal wants as best they could.

The latest of the old Mexican records shows about

twenty thousand baptized, registered Indians. It is doubtful whether more than two-thirds of this number were actually attached to the missions in the sense of having permanent homes upon them. During the fifteen years which elapsed between the final dismemberment of the missions and the acquisition of California by the United States in 1848, it is safe to say that about half of the Mission Indians were driven from their lands by venturesome Mexicans who coveted their valuable homes. However accurate this estimate may be, the United States Government found in its new domain some seven thousand of these Indians still peacefully occupying the old mission lands, and cultivating the same parcels which had been the homes of their fathers and grandfathers before them. The earliest United States Government report of the Mission Indians appears in 1851:

"At the close of the Mexican war some of these old Mission Indians remained in possession of lands under written grants from the Mexican Government. Some have sold out, others have been elbowed off by white men. All are now waiting the adjudication of the commissioner of land titles. Many of them are good citizens in all respects save the right to vote and be witnesses. They are anxious to hold their title homesteads and resist all offers to buy as steadily as they can. How long their limited shrewdness can match the overreaching cupidity that ever assails them it is difficult to say.

The Indian Dispossessed

" They lack thrift, incline to dissolute habits, yet plant regularly year by year, and have small stocks of horses, cattle, and sheep. A better crop and more commodious huts, a few chairs, and a table distinguish them from the mountain villages; still, they have made a broad step towards civilization. Custom has always allowed them ardent spirits, from which lamentable practice not even the missionaries can be excepted. The laws of nature have had their course, and the Indian is paying the penalty of all who violate them. Three years ago they were practically slaves. American freedom does not profit them. They soon fall into the bad ways of their Christian neighbors. American rule and American liberty, which have come to them and overthrown the church, have given them the white man's habits of dissipation, and they are disgusted with prospects of civilized life."

Sixty years of Franciscan dominion had served to differentiate these Indians from all other Indians in the great western country; they presented an aspect of Indian life entirely new to the advancing hosts of Uncle Sam. But sixty years under paternal guardianship had left them unassertive, dependent without those upon whom to depend, and wholly unprepared to cope with the persistent American frontiersman. The system from which they had derived their great benefits developed rather than overcame the Indians' one great weakness, — their child-like dependence upon the guiding hand of a stronger people.

" Wherever, in California," says one of the earlier Government reports, " an Indian is discovered superior to the mass of his fellows, it will be found, with scarce an exception, that he speaks Spanish (not English), from which it may be safely inferred that he was once attached to some mission. There is about the same difference between these Mission Indians and the wild tribes as there is between the educated American negro and a wild African; these have both undergone the same process, and with very nearly the same results."

If the Mission Indian question appeared to the Government as a novel one, the attitude of the Government toward the Mission Indians was no less unique. From the earliest times it had been the custom of the Government to recognize in the wild, nomadic tribes a possessory right to their vast hunting-grounds which required extinguishment by treaty and by purchase. For a more or less (usually less) valuable consideration the aborigines had been induced to recede before the white population, but always with at least the color of a bargain.

But the rights of the Mission Indians were summarily disposed of in an astonishing manner by this decision of a committee of the United States Senate: " that the United States, acquiring possession of the territory from Mexico, succeeded to its rights in the soil; and as that Government regarded itself as the absolute and unqualified owner of it, and held that the Indian had no usufructuary or other rights therein which were to be in any manner respected, they, the United States, were under no obligations to treat with the Indians occupying the same for the extinguishment of their title." Thus it happened that the Indians, who had, according to generally accepted views as to the rights acquired by long-continued occupancy and cultivation, the best right of all Indians to the land of their ancestors, were to receive from the Government not even the color of recognition. In all the great book of Indian treaties, there is not one treaty or agreement with the Mission Indians. They had nothing for which to treat.

Under these conditions the Mission Indians were delivered to the tender mercies of the never-to-be-stopped pioneer at a time when great discoveries of placer gold had brought hordes of more than usually adventurous and reckless prospectors into the new country. No attitude of the Government toward the Indians could have better pleased the on-coming white men.

" In accordance with this view," writes a special commissioner, " the assumed Indian title has always been disregarded by the land-officers of the Government in this district, and by settlers. As expressed by the present register of the land-office, the location of an Indian family or families on land upon which a white man desires to settle is, in law, no more a bar to such settlement than would be the presence of a stray sheep or cow. And so, like sheep or cattle, they have been too often driven from their homes and their cultivated fields, the Government, through its officers, refusing to hear their protests, as though in equity as well as in law they had no rights in the least deserving consideration."

The story of the Mission Indians is best told in the annual reports of the Indian Office. It is a tale too incredible to be told in any other way.

" The Coahuilas, of San Timoteo, during the existence of the smallpox two or three years ago, fled in dismay, leaving their lands, not with the intention of abandoning them, but from fear of the epidemic. The white settlers near the Indian lands immediately took forcible possession of them, and have positively refused to give them up. It is of the utmost importance that immediate steps be taken to examine fully into this matter, to the end that strict and impartial justice be done in the premises. . . .

" Some nine miles from Temecula is a place called Pajamo. When the Indians left this place for their summer grounds, a number of villainous Americans, headed by two men named Breeze and Woolfe, burned the Indian houses or ' jacablo,' and then took forcible possession of their lands and ditches. This is the complaint made by the Indians, and it is substantiated by the whites. Justice demands a full and impartial investigation of this matter. . . .

"During the last year, in several instances, the whites have induced Indians to abandon their little farms for the purpose of obtaining possession themselves; as an inducement giving them trifling presents. I told the Indians, by doing so, they could never again occupy their lands, and consequently would be without homes for their families, and told them they ought not to sell or give up their farms to any one.

"The fact is, however, the whites are pushing back on the frontier, and unless lands are reserved for the use of the Indians, soon they will have no place to live. . . .

"I have been acting as special agent for the Mission and Coahuila Indians five years, and during that time have forwarded to the Commissioner of Indian Affairs at Washington detailed reports of the conditions and wants of the Indians of Southern California, showing the number and locality of each tribe, recommending the establishment of a reservation to which the Indians could be taken as they became crowded out of their homes by the white settlers.

"I presume that one reason why nothing has been done for these Indians is, they have been peaceable and caused the Government no trouble, and consequently have been almost entirely neglected."

The Mission Indians

Every report urges the necessity of reserves for the Mission Indians, to include especially the lands on which their villages are located. Naturally, every instinct of the voting white population opposed such a waste of the public domain. But finally, after *twenty years*, the first Indian reserve was set apart for the Mission Indians, — a large tract in the San Pasqual Valley, including the Indian village, or rancheria, of San Pasqual. The frantic demonstrations of the outraged settlers against this usurpation of their right to the whole country are more than hinted at in the agent's report:

"On the 2d of April, 1870, the reservation order was received, and the office of the agency was moved to San Pasqual Valley reservation, when I learned that the settlers had employed counsel to have the order set aside, had also enlisted the sympathy and co-operation of the majority of the people of the county in their favor, and that the editors of San Diego were publishing some most wonderful curiosities in the way of newspaper incendiary literature, in no manner calculated to throw oil on the troubled waters. I also found the Indians had been told 'they were to be made slaves of by the Government; smallpox was to be introduced in the clothing sent them; their cattle were to be taken from them;' and to such an extent had they been tampered with, that they positively refused to locate on the lands set apart and secured for their especial

The Indian Dispossessed

use and benefit. The parties tampering with the Indians I have classified as follows:

" 1st, settlers on the reservations; 2d, settlers in the vicinage; 3d, men living with Indian women; 4th, persons employing Indian labor at little or no wages; 5th, politicians after votes; 6th, lawyers after fees in contingency; 7th, vagabonds generally. I can safely assert that not one in the above-enumerated classes has the true interests of the Indian at heart, but is actuated by motives personal or those of a friend. . . .

" The Indian law prevailing in this agency is exceedingly doubtful, uncertain, and unjust in its workings. The townships contiguous to the reservations, viz., Agua Caliente, Temecula, and Santa Isabel, have no justices of the peace, and have had none for many years. It does appear to me that there is a chronic indisposition on the part of the people of Southern California to having a duly constituted judiciary. The nearest court of justice is in one direction, San Luis Rey, some twenty miles, and in San Diego, about thirty-four miles. I would therefore recommend that some provision of law may be devised whereby the agent may be empowered to exercise the functions of a justice of the peace, and that something similar to a garrison or regimental court might be authorized for the trial of light offences, the captains and principal men to compose the court, the findings of said court to be submitted to the agent for his approval, or otherwise.

"The settlers on the reservation are making no preparations to move on the 1st of September proximo, as ordered by the superintendent of Indian affairs, State of California. As all the available land is taken up by the settlers on the reservations, I would respectfully ask, Where am I to locate the Indians if they should conclude to come in after this date? . . .

"San Pasqual rancheria, on San Pasqual Valley reservation, is located on less than a quarter-section of land; even this is partitioned among the settlers, who are only restrained by fear of the Government from taking possession at once and driving the Indians therefrom."

The story of San Pasqual Village is typical of all the Mission Indian rancherias. The agent's serious statement of the conditions there counted as nothing against the efforts of the Vociferous Few. Did ever the vote-seeking Uncle Sam let pass unheeded the clamor of his Chosen? Within a year the President revoked the order establishing the Indian reserve, and once more the gentle white man was at liberty to push the Indian further up into the canyons. In the next report the agent recounts the manner of it:

"San Pasqual and Pala were established as Indian pueblos under the secularization law of 1834.

These lands had long been occupied by the Christian Indians, and in 1835 were divided among them by the priests and prefect in accordance with said laws, and were occupied by them until dispossessed by squatters within the last few years. . . .

" The possessory claim of the Indians to land has never been deemed a serious impediment to white settlers; the latter always take by force that which they fail to obtain by persuasion.

" Conceiving that this state of things would ultimately leave the Mission Indians homeless, I recommended in my annual report for 1869 ' that certain lands at Pala and San Pasqual Valleys, in San Diego County, which had been given to the Indians by the Mexican Government, be removed from public sale, surveyed, and set apart as a reservation.' I stated ' that the Indian claims to these lands had never been presented to the board of land commissioners appointed under the act of 1851 to settle private land claims in California, and were consequently disregarded by the settlers, the lands being presumptively a part of the public domain.'

" On the 31st of January, 1870, pursuant to this recommendation and a similar suggestion made by J. B. McIntosh, then acting as superintendent of Indian Affairs for California, the President of the United States made an order setting apart those lands for an Indian reservation, and a proclamation was issued to that effect.

The Mission Indians

" The settlers, coveting the valleys, formed an organization against this movement. They employed counsel at home and in Washington to draw up and present to our Representatives in Congress and the President of the United States papers falsifying facts, for the purpose of obtaining a revocation of the order.

" I am informed by Indians, and by white men of great respectability, that a notorious monte-dealer by the name of McCan, residing at New San Diego, prepared a remonstrance against the reservation, and, with the assistance of two others, attached to it several hundred names (Indian and Mexican), and transmitted it to Washington. Some of these names were collected from old church records, and were the names of Indians and Mexicans who had been dead for years; and none of them, if I am correctly informed, were written or authorized by the parties to whom they belonged. McCan subsequently boasted of his success, and the facility with which so many signatures and marks could be made by three scribes only. For this valuable service McCan received $40 from Olegario, $20 from Manuel Largo, and smaller sums from various other mountain Indians, who had become, through false representations of the settlers, opposed to a reservation. This, with other documents of a kindred nature, was taken to Washington by Ben. C. Truman, and on the 17th day of February, 1871, the order of the President was revoked, and the special agent for the Mission Indians soon after dismissed."

Did this recital rouse the Government to a restoration of the Indian lands? Did ever recitals of fiendish acts in the Indian country stir the Government to any action opposed to the wishes of the almighty voter?

Two years later another special agent continues the sad story of San Pasqual:

" I reached San Pasqual on the 15th instant, from Pawai, where you were yourself detained. I proceeded at once to the house of Panto Lion, captain of the village, and requested him to summon his people together on the following morning for a conference, at the same time explaining to him that we had been sent by the Government at Washington to inquire into their condition and to ascertain if anything could be done by the Government to aid them.

" The villagers began to assemble early. At the appointed hour the captain rose, and in a short speech in the Indian language, which seemed to be both eloquent and well appreciated, gave his hearers to understand the errand upon which I visited them. A lively interest was manifested by every one. They complained of the encroachments of their American neighbors upon their land, and pointed to a house near by, built by one of the more adventurous of his class, who claimed to have pre-empted the land upon which the larger part of the village lies. On calling upon the man afterward, I found that such was really the case, and that he had actually paid the price of the land to the register of the land-office of this district, and was daily expecting the patent from Washington. He owned it was hard to wrest from these well-disposed and industrious creatures the homes they had built up. ' But,' said he, ' if I had not done it somebody else would, for all agree that the Indian has no right to public lands.' These Indians further complain that settlers take advantage of them in every way possible; employ them to work and insist on paying them in trifles that are of no account to them; ' dock ' them for imaginary neglect, or fail entirely to pay them; take up their stock on the slightest pretext and make exorbitant charges for damages and detention of the stock seized. They are in many cases unable to redeem it. They have therefore little encouragement to work or to raise stock. Nor do they care to plant fruit-trees or grapevines as long as land thus improved may be taken from them, as has been the case in very many instances. Among the little homes included in the pre-emption claim above referred to are those adorned with trees and vines. Instead of feeling secure and happy in the possession of what little is left to them, they are continually filled with anxiety. They claim that they ought to be allowed to remain where their forefathers have lived for so long, and that they should be protected by law in the peaceful possession of the homes that have been handed down to them.

" I asked how they would like for their children to go to school, learn to speak the English language, and to live more like white people. It would be very nice, they replied, but it would do them little good if they could not have their homes protected.

" I asked them how they would like to be moved to some place where they would be better protected, have ground of their own secured to them, and more comfortable homes. The answer was, ' Our fathers lived and died here, and we would rather live here than at any other place.' "

Two years more, and another agent writes:

" The valleys of San Pasqual and Pala, in San Diego County, which were once set apart for a reservation would afford good homes for a large part of the people, *and ought to be restored to them.* The abolishment of this reservation four years ago was secured by interested parties, through a shameful perversion and falsification of the real facts of the case at that time, and the Indians yet remaining in these valleys are being shamefully imposed upon by the settlers."

Then San Pasqual disappears from the records for a period of several years. It has officially ceased to exist. But in 1883 a special commissioner writes the final chapter:

The Mission Indians

"This San Pasqual village was a regularly organized Indian pueblo, formed by about one hundred neophytes of the San Luis Rey Mission, under and in accordance with the provisions of the Secularization Act in 1834. The record of its founding is preserved in the Mexican archives at San Francisco. . . . There is now, on the site of that old Indian pueblo, a white settlement numbering thirty-five voters. The Indians are all gone, — some to other villages; some living near by in canyons and nooks in the hills, from which, on the occasional visits of the priest, they gather and hold services in the half-ruined adobe chapel built by them in the days of their prosperity."

Vale, San Pasqual!

From a superficial point of view one might be led to think that the Government delighted to witness the slow extinction of Indians at the hands of the Faithful. It is really not so. The officials of the Government have never been disposed to inflict unnecessary torture on the receding Indian. But their very official existence depends upon the pleasure, not of the whole people whom they are supposed to represent, but of the few who are sufficiently interested in legislation to *express* their pleasure or displeasure. There is no virtue, in the official mind, in the *unexpressed* sentiment of a great order- and justice-loving people, so long as they continue to live under the delusion that the public servants are directing the public business with due regard for the national honor.

Thus it is that the Vociferous Few — they may be attending the vanishing Indian in the West, or gathered upon velvet in the effete East — besmirch the whole official mass, and color national legislation with their filthy desires. The public servants can-not, under the Constitution, get above the level of their rulers.

While the San Pasqual tragedy was being en-acted, a similar affair was attempted on another California reservation which illustrates well the prevailing conditions:

" By order of the Commissioner of Indian Affairs, I caused two suits to be commenced for trespass on lands inside of the reservation fence. I expected to be able to test the validity of *swamp*-land claims to some of the best *wheat*-land now cultivated on the reservation. Lobby influence at Washington was too much for the Indian Department. A telegraph-order from the United States Attorney-General's Office to L. D. Latimer, United States district at-torney, directed that officer to suspend all further proceedings against trespassers on the Round Valley reserve. . . .

" The Indian Department has in actual possession and under fence only about 4,000 acres, and a por-tion of that is falsely claimed as swamp-land. The balance of the valley is in possession of settlers, all clamorous for breaking up the reservation and driving the Indians away.

"It is useless to attempt to disguise the fact that, so long as these settlers have a voice in the selection of our Representatives to Congress, and Indians have none, they must and will be heard at Washington. I would say, listen to them, and if they propose a fair compromise of a vexed question, accede to it; but if they are fully determined to drive the red man from the face of the earth, without a hearing, and without bread or money, stop them in their mad career, and say, 'Thus far shalt thou go, and no farther.' There can be no doubt that it is the duty of Congress to act in this matter with promptness and fidelity; and to delay action would be criminal."

"Thus far shalt thou go, and no farther." Impossible language in the land of the Free. It suggests a curtailment of personal freedom. A Government slavishly dependent upon the expressed will of the people has no incentive to enforce a sustained, consistent Indian policy opposed to *local* interests, although in accord with the perfectly well understood, but unexpressed, sentiment of the *great body* of the American people. It cannot afford to sacrifice political capital by administering a richly deserved rebuke in one quarter, unless it thereby makes an equal or greater gain in another quarter. To be sure, the public generously applauds a righteous act in the Indian country, but the public remembers for a day, while the interested few remember until election day. To this psychological fact may be charged most of the vicious legislation which afflicts the American people.

The effect of this political cowardice upon the trespassing settlers is pictured in the same report:

" Since the order of the United States Attorney-General to suspend all legal proceedings against certain trespassers on the Round Valley reservation, some of them have become bold and insolent. Gates and fences have been frequently thrown open. Indian lodges, established at the gates for the convenience of travellers wishing to cross the reservation, and for the protection of growing crops, have been wantonly broken up by ruffians. The Indians have been driven off, and outside stock wickedly turned into the reservation inclosures, there to riot in growing wheat, oats, and corn, some of which was nearly ripe enough to cut. There are many respectable settlers in the valley who abhor this conduct, and would gladly see the culprits brought to a just punishment. It is not, however, considered a safe undertaking, in the neighborhood of Indian reservations in California, for a good, law-abiding man to attempt to punish a bad man and a law-breaker by habit for any indignity to Indians or those having them in charge. . . .

" A soldier recently murdered an Indian in his

bed, on the Hoopa reservation. It is said to have been done without the slightest provocation. No redress can be had in Klamath County. Grand juries have repeatedly refused to take any notice of complaints where it is alleged that a white man killed or committed any other wrong upon an Indian.

" It is no longer a mooted question whether bad white men, wilful trespassers, liquor-dealers, murderers, thieves, and outlaws shall be kept off and away from the reservations, but rather, shall the reservations be permitted or kept up at all?

" It is not considered a crime to steal horses and cattle in Round Valley, so long as they are taken from the Indian reservation."

This was the condition of Indian affairs in California twenty-five years after the United States Government had rescued the country from the tyranny of Mexico.

Why did not the Indian, in this land where " all men are created equal," possess himself of the magic vote and become one of the Chosen? It may seem incredible that any Indian should have had the temerity to face the conditions which surrounded the precious ballot, but the fact is officially recorded in this twenty-fifth year:

" Three Indians at least have recently made application to be registered as citizens in Los Angeles County. Their petition was refused by the clerk of the county court, acting under the advice of the district attorney, on the sole ground of their being Indians. They then referred the matter, through their attorney, C. N. Wilson, Esq., to the United States Commissioner at Los Angeles, asking him to take such action in the premises as would fully test their rights in this regard under the Constitution. He refused to have anything to do with the case, further than to transmit the affidavits of the Indians to the district attorney at San Francisco. Here the matter rests for the present, with little prospect that anything in their interest will be done by the officers of justice to whom they have made appeal."

Year after year the story of the Mission Indians appears in the official reports:

"I may first remark, in general, that I find them a much more numerous, civilized, and industrious people than I had supposed; properly provided for, their future is hopeful. Their relation to the Government, and the white population now pressing in upon them, is a sad commentary upon the Christian civilization of the age in its modes of dealing with the weak and defenceless. If citizens, their rights as such have been entirely overlooked and trampled upon; if wards of the Government, they have been most sadly neglected, left at the mercy and in the power of the citizens who are settling around and among them. While some treat them humanely, yet the too prevailing sentiment is that they have no rights which a white man is bound to respect, while the general testimony is that they are singularly loyal to the Government, honest, peaceable, inoffensive, and patient under wrongs. Among all the dependent wards of the Government there are none so much needing or deserving her speedy and fostering care; and to relieve them from their present deplorable condition will be a truly humane and Christian work. . . .

"The one pressing want of these people now is land, on which they can cultivate their gardens, herd their stock, and feel secure in the possession of their homes. At every place I have visited, their homes are being invaded by settlers with their stock. In one settlement, Morongo, in San Bernardino County, the people have all been driven off at the point of the revolver. Everywhere the sad complaint is that their gardens are being invaded and their pastures consumed by the stock of settlers; the water turned away from their ditches to irrigate the gardens of those trespassing upon their lands; and they have no redress. And I know from observation that their complaints are but too true. This state of things cannot continue much longer without disastrous consequences. Either these helpless, non-resisting people will be driven from their lands as homeless wanderers, or will be exasperated to violent deeds of self-defence. Then we know what will follow. I cannot exaggerate the urgency of this case. Something must be done soon, or at least reliable assurances must be given that the Government will adjust difficulties. What can be done? In my judgment, it is no use to spend any more money or time in sending commissioners or agents to talk; Indians and settlers alike say they have had enough of this, and I feel I do not want to go again among that people without authority to do, or at least propose, something in the way of a speedy and safe settlement of these grave difficulties."

But "sending commissioners or agents to talk" disturbed no political fences, and soothed the Government's conscience with the notion that it was doing something, while it shrank from sustaining the Indian rights, and dreaded as well to complete the sacrifice of the Indian for political gain.

Poor, buffeted, helpless Uncle Sam! The servant of the people, the tool of the Vociferous Few! So the miserable business of "sending commissioners" went on. After thirty years of existence under the "Banner of Freedom," the Mission Indians received the distinguished consideration of another very complete report of their unfortunate condition:

"The Mission Indians may be divided, with respect to their condition and manner of living, into three classes. The first division may be defined as those who stay on or about the ranches or farms of white men, living by daily labor upon the farms, receiving, when they work, about one dollar per

The Mission Indians

day. Most of the larger ranchmen have about them one or several families, whom they permit to build their slight houses on the corners of the ranch, or on grounds adjoining, and in addition allow the use of water sufficient to irrigate a garden, which such Indians often cultivate. These Indians do most of the ordinary work of the ranches, except when harvest-time, sheep-shearing, or some special season requires the employment of other help. They live more or less comfortably, as the proprietor of the ranch to which they are attached is a humane and just man, or hard-hearted and a cheat. They are not legal tenants; they cannot make legal contracts, or collect their wages by a suit at law, if for no other reason, because they have not the means to prosecute suits. The interests of the ranchman generally dictate treatment at least fair enough to prevent his Indians from moving away from him. This class of Indians is pretty large. They have no difficulty in securing enough food and comfortable clothing, and some of them have learned to be thrifty and prudent.

" The second class is made up of those who live in small communities, cultivating lands they have held for a long time and have been accustomed to call their own. At each village are gathered as many families as the natural supply of water will make comfortable. They desire above all else to be left in possession of these little villages, which

The Indian Dispossessed

are situated wherever a spring or small stream of water exists, scattered through a large tract of otherwise desert country. Thus they have a village at Potrero, twenty-five miles from here. Twenty miles in another direction is another village; fifteen miles farther another village, and so on. Till recently all these places were on unsurveyed public lands, and unclaimed. Now white men have set up claims of more or less valid character upon almost every acre of these lands, and they are liable to be taken away unless there is prompt and energetic action by the Government. Each Indian family at these villages has a house and cultivates a patch of ground, varying from one acre to four or five. A field of five acres cultivated by one family is rarely found. Fruit-trees and well-kept vines are not unusual. The Indian men plant their fields in the spring, give them a more or less thrifty cultivation till a season comes when they can get temporary employment on ranches, and then they leave their homes in charge of the squaws and old men, and go out to labor, very much as the young men in Canada flock over into 'the States' in haying-time to work for the New England and New York farmers. A much greater number of the Mission Indians were formerly included in this class, and oftentimes the Indians described in the first class owned and cultivated the very lands where they are now only tolerated as day-laborers. They

228

are very much attached to their homes. One Indian that I know has maintained a home in the Potrero, and for many years worked most of the time twenty miles away. He is as little willing to give up his Potrero house and field as any of his neighbors who live there constantly. But now his home is threatened by a land-grabber who wants it for nothing. This second class of Indians are the ones now most especially needing the energetic care of the Government. The land-grabbers are after them, and an agent with seven-leagued boots could scarcely travel from village to village as fast as those Americans who are seeking a few acres of ground with a spring upon it, or moist lands where wheat and potatoes grow without irrigation, that may be pre-empted or taken up under the desert-land act. That such lands have been held by Indians and cultivated by Indians counts for nothing more than if they had been only homes for grasshoppers and coyotes. This seems to me a great and unpardonable vice in the law, that it treats as unoccupied, and subject to pre-emption, lands which have been in fact occupied and cultivated precisely as white men occupy and cultivate, and that, too, for more than one generation of living men. But for that vice of the law the Mission Indians would now be secure in their old possessions, and where their improvements and water-rights were wanted they would be bought and paid for instead of taken for nothing in the name of law. I cannot learn at all accurately the number of this class of Indians, but do not suppose they can be more than one-third of all.

"The third class is rather small, and includes those that hang upon the outskirts of towns, pass wistfully through the streets, seldom asking for anything, but silently begging with their longing, pathetic eyes. At times, when they can get whisky, the men are besotted brutes, and the women are generally prostitutes, though the family tie is still strong enough to keep squaw and papoose with the husband. With this class are some unmarried women who are prostitutes. This, which I will call the vagrant class, is not so large as I was prepared to find it; and I believe, from observation and from general report, that vagrancy is not a state into which the Mission Indians naturally or willingly fall. Except in the third class, I believe prostitution is almost or quite unknown, and that the virtue of women is quite as highly esteemed and as much practiced as among the most enlightened peoples."

Neither does the report of 1880 show any change in the settled habits of the frontiersmen:

"Those who by sufferance have lands to cultivate where they live, have tilled them to profit during the season. Only yesterday two Indians from the San Luis Rey tribe called at the agency, reporting that they had come with two wagons, loaded with over seven thousand pounds of wheat, which they were having ground into flour for sale and for their own use. This amount the two men had raised by their own labor; and they report that their people have plenty of wheat and are doing well.

"It is doubtful, however, whether they will be allowed to gather another harvest from those fields which they have long cultivated, and which, until recently, they believed to be reserved lands. Two years ago a 'land-grabber' suddenly discovered that these Indians were not on the lands reserved for them in a given township east of the meridian line, but in the corresponding township west of the meridian, and at once filed upon the land they occupied under the 'desert-land act.' How lands cultivated by these people for more than a generation can be called 'desert' I am not able to answer. But it is quite likely that certain land officials in these parts who consider the occupancy of lands by Indians as of no more significance than their occupancy by so many coyotes will have less difficulty with such questions. The Indian 'must go' if he is on a patch of ground that a white man wants, and no matter that he has lived on and cultivated it for a generation. It is wanted all the more on account of its improved condition. . . .

"Other wrongs practiced upon these helpless people

have been checked in great measure since my arrival at this agency, such as the fraudulent methods of employers in paying Indian laborers. Every conceivable trick is resorted to to get labor of this kind as cheap as possible. The following case was brought to my attention some time ago. An Indian having labored at cutting wood for six days, earning, at the wages agreed upon, the sum of $2.50, received in part payment two bottles of wine, for which he was charged $1, and upon demanding the balance of $1.50 in money he was ordered to leave the premises. The Indian refusing to go without his money, the man took down his shot-gun and discharged a load of buck-shot into the Indian's face, destroying the sight of an eye and otherwise disfiguring his face. The next day this employer boasted to an acquaintance how he had settled a bill of $1.50 with an Indian by paying him in buck-shot."

And in the following year:

" A further source of trouble in this connection is that growing out of the fact that even-numbered sections have been reserved for Indians within the limits of ' railroad land grants.' In some instances their villages are found to be on railroad sections; or, if they happen to be on reserved land, their little fields, cultivated all these years, are claimed as within the limits of the railroad grant, their improvements presenting such temptations as to overcome all considerations of sympathy and right. The lands are entered in the office of the railroad company, taken and occupied, and the Indians turned out. Now if the same rights which attach in common to the *bonâ fide* white settler occupying land prior to such grant to railroads were accorded to Indian occupants, it would be different; but, unfortunately for the Indian, he has not yet in *fact* come to be considered by the Government as a *man,* although bearing the impress of a common Maker in all respects except as to the color of his skin. . . .

" Referring to the subject of civilization, I have to say that the Mission Indians are as much civilized as the population by which they are surrounded; and if they are not up to the full standard, it is because of their surroundings. All wear civilized dress, sustain themselves, with few exceptions, by civilized pursuits, and hold themselves answerable to the law of the land when they violate it."

However lightly this constant tale of woe may have affected Congress, its reactive effect on one of the agents was marked. After four years of service as compiler of facts for the dusty archives of the Government, he vents his disgust:

" It is true the goal of my ambition to see them provided with land for permanent homes, which has been so persistently urged in former reports, has not yet been reached. And my faith in the power and influence of agents' reports and letters on subjects of this nature is at this writing very much shaken by results, or, rather, the want of results. But I have not been alone in efforts in this direction, nor yet in want of success. Since my last annual report voluntary and independent action has been taken by a prominent State religious and city-trade association, as well as by prominent individuals, in the way of memorializing Congress in behalf of homes for these people, but with no better result. To me it is doubtful whether Congress will ever take action in the premises, since it has been demonstrated in its past dealings with the Indian question that distinguished consideration is shown to the Indian only in proportion as he has developed a disposition to be troublesome and worthless."

But here is a variation from the usual tale:

" In the month of June last I visited a village of the San Luis Rey Indians, who had hitherto been wandering about, landless and homeless, but who a year ago settled in the foot-hills near Temecula ranch, from which they were once ejected. No running water is found where they live, but at great labor they had dug wells and developed water for domestic purposes. They had just harvested their first crops, consisting of wheat and barley, which was grown upon winter rains. One Indian told me he would have about 500 sacks of barley. I estimated that they would have about two carloads of grain to sell over and above what they would require for their own use. The land they had settled upon I found to be surveyed Government land, and I found also that their success in growing grain upon it had already attracted the attention of the ubiquitous ' land grabber.' No time must be lost in securing this land for these Indians. The Indians feared they might be driven off, and I promised them I would not sleep after returning to the agency till I had written to Washington and asked that this land be given to them. I kept my promise, and, with commendable promptness, I received an executive order setting apart the land for their use. To me, as well as to these Indians, it was the most gratifying incident of the year."

It is indeed something that the Indian's refuge in the canyons was saved to him. The case of this little band of San Luis Rey Indians was only one of many. In foot-hills, in canyons, on unclaimed little oases in the deserts — wherever a few of the dispossessed Indians had gathered together in the hope of again establishing themselves — executive orders were secured setting aside portions of the public domain for their use. And whenever one of these little reservations proved too tempting to the on-coming white man, he had only to persist in his inalienable right to the pursuit of happiness in that particular spot; another executive order as easily disposed of the Indian right, and restored the land to the public domain — to *his* domain. The real significance of the Government's beneficence is disclosed in the report for 1886:

" The Government has apparently been very generous to the Mission Indians. It has given them more than twenty different reservations, embracing nearly 200,000 acres; but what a country! After a careful examination of all the land we do not think there are over 5,000 acres of tillable land, and the best portion of that is now held by trespassers in defiance of the agent and Government.

" The Potrero reservation is covered over with squatters who have settled there long since the lands were set apart for Indian purposes. They are there in open defiance of law. They have managed to get their cases before the Indian Department for adjudication. The rights of these Indians to these lands are as clear and absolute as the proclamation of a President can make them. The squatters should never have had a standing in court till after they were dispossessed. The Government ought to have removed every one of them, and if they have rights then let them assert them before the courts. Until the Indians feel assured of a perfect title they will not build houses, put out orchards or vineyards, nor anything to make the land more valuable."

" The squatters should " and " the Government ought " — these are sure marks of a new agent. What a godsend to his Government and to the Indians each and every new, inexperienced agent fondly imagines himself! The grossest, most palpable injustices have only awaited his coming, that a simple recital of self-evident abuses with their equally patent remedies (strange that previous agents have overlooked them!) shall bring happiness out of misery and order out of chaos.

Poor fellow! He soon discovers himself — a mere speck in the political firmament, just below the horizon. The squatter continues to do as he pleases, and the great Government continues to do as the squatter pleases.

After forty years of wild and reckless " Freedom " at the expense of the miserable Mission Indians, the squatters met their first — and only — reverse. The great Government automaton suddenly refused to respond to invisible political pulls. Its executive head — horrible discovery! — had the temerity to respond to impulses from his own nerve-centres.

" The position of these intruders," proclaimed President Grover Cleveland, " is one of simple and bare-faced wrong-doing, plainly questioning the inclination of the Government to protect its dependent Indian wards and its ability to maintain itself in the guaranty of such protection. These intruders should forthwith feel the weight of the Government's power."

This expressed the attitude of the Cleveland administration toward the persecuted Indian. A short time previous to this declaration the removal of the astonished squatters had been undertaken, with varying success. One agent reports the accomplishment of squatter removals without serious difficulty, and adds, " What these men will do under the circumstances I know not. They have been seeking relief through their representatives in Congress, but the result is not reported."

Far more interesting is the account from the Round Valley reservation. It was here that, fifteen years before, suits of ejectment had been summarily dismissed because " Lobby influence at Washington was too much for the Indian Department." In this year, 1887, as in 1872, the trespassers were firmly entrenched behind their local political forces; they met the Government order for removal with a prompt refusal; they unhesitatingly arrayed themselves against Federal authority, and Federal authority bravely undertook to vindicate itself by calling into requisition a section of its little army. It is a comedy briefly but concisely told in telegraphic despatches between Gen. O. O. Howard, commanding the Department of the Pacific, and the War Department. General Howard opens the play:

" . . . Captain Shaw's company, First Artillery, was, August 17, sent to evict trespassers upon Round Valley Indian reservation. On 19th instant he commenced evictions and was thereupon served with injunction, issued by Judge Superior Court of Mendocino County, California, by person claiming to be deputy sheriff of same, which Captain Shaw refused to obey, and continued to evict. Upon affidavit of said deputy sheriff, judge of said court has issued attachment for Shaw, who declined to surrender. . . ."

Plucky man, Captain Shaw. He seems to have labored under the impression that his Government had some rights which the Vociferous Few were bound to respect.

The next day General Howard again telegraphed the Department:

"Shall I leave Captain Shaw to be arrested and imprisoned, at the call of the trespassers, who have no rights whatever, in obedience to orders of local courts? . . . Please sustain me, and Captain Shaw, who has not exceeded our orders one whit."

And the War Department replied to the General:

"In view of facts as presented to the Secretary of War, he directs that you desist in declining to obey writ until question of jurisdiction is determined by Federal courts."

So the soldier boys wended their way homeward, carrying their wounded feelings with them, while the squatters held high carnival, victors upon a bloodless field; in the doleful language of the Commissioner of Indian Affairs, "Thus the second attempt to regain possession of the reservation by military force ended in utter failure."

"All Government derives its just powers from the

consent of the governed " — therefore, if the governed do not consent, they have only to cry, " Hands off! " and the Government may only view from the outside their unique efforts to govern themselves.

The spectacle of Round Valley is not an unusual one. Nothing short of a general and bloody riot, threatening destruction under conditions manifestly beyond all local control, will induce the American people to tolerate the interference of the Federal Government, so grounded are they in the belief that their full measure of " life, liberty, and the pursuit of happiness " can come only through the sacred right of each and every community to be a " law unto itself " in its local affairs. The scheme of " Government by the people " does not contemplate a central authority which shall exercise a salutary control over widely diverse social conditions in the interest of a homogeneous and consistent whole. A community has only to fortify itself with its own public sentiment that, in the pursuit of happiness, Indians may be driven to the deserts, or negro citizens burned at the stake; that community is as secure from Federal interference as would be any neighboring Spanish-American State that might indulge in similar pastimes. More secure, for if an American negro citizen were to be burned alive in any country on the face of the globe except his own, one of the most efficient navies afloat would enforce, if necessary, full and prompt reparation for the outrage. Uncle Sam is impotent only within his own realm.

And the story of the Mission Indians goes on in the annual reports:

" The teachings of the padres saved them from savagism. Neglect and white man's greed have robbed them of land, and his vices have reduced their numbers from 15,000 in 1834, to 7,000 in 1852, to 3,000 in 1890. No man with a particle of humanity left can meet these people as an agent does without feeling ashamed as the agent of this good Government, which has forcibly taken possession of this country and assumed the care for this weak people, that we should have by neglect and dishonesty of its paid agents reduced them to such abject poverty and helplessness. Our own records of the past are humiliating. Cortez robbed the Aztecs of gold, but left them their land and water. Americans posing as Christians have robbed these poor children of nature, by legal trickery, of their land made sacred by the graves of their ancestors. As agent for this Government, that I know desires to deal fairly with this people, now I ask and urge that a commissioner may be appointed to come here and settle all land titles, give these people from ten to twenty acres of available land with water for homes, tools to work with, and enforce attendance in school until every child has secured a common

The Indian Dispossessed

English education. In this way we can soon make some return for the lands we have driven them from, and make them self-supporting, intelligent, local citizens. Oft-repeated promises and disappointments cause them to distrust any statement made by civil officers, with reason."

Here again, in 1894, are the San Pasqual Indians, after many years in oblivion:

"*San Pasqual Village.* These Indians have been treated by the United States in a very unfair and unjust manner. Their lands in San Pasqual Valley were granted to them by the Mexican Government. Notwithstanding this, the United States patented the same lands to whites, and, as a result, the Indians had to leave and seek a new home, which, when found, does not in the slightest compare with their former lands in San Pasqual Valley. They are quiet, law-abiding people, and deserve consideration at the hands of the Government."

1848–1898. Fifty years under the glorious flag of the United States. In this year, 1898, did the Mission Indians celebrate the semi-centennial with a grand jubilee, or joyously sing, " My country 't is of thee, sweet land of liber*tee*, of thee I sing " ? If they did, there is no record of it. The agent's report for that year mentions no singing:

" Once they possessed the best of this land, in fact, owned it all. The advent of the white man has resulted in their discomfiture, and they have

242

The Mission Indians

been driven back to inhospitable canyons, gravelly wastes, and mountain-tops. In this position we find them to-day, humiliated, and in many cases legally robbed of their former possessions. The protection of their remaining rights from the rapacity of the whites, even to the pillaging of the little feed that grows within the confines of their reservation, is a task of no small magnitude.

" While upon this subject it would be *à propos* to consider the self-support of these people. I desire to call your attention forcibly to this fact, that they are not in any sense of the term self-supporting. In a majority of instances they are geographically located so that self-support is impossible. Without soil or water, they are obliged to depend upon the acorn and mesquite bean crop and other forage for their subsistence."

Then the nineteenth century draws to a close; the American people have become one of the greatest of the world's nations. They have expanded to the farthest limits of their great country. California has added her scores of millions of golden treasure to the national wealth and her old Mission lands have yielded their millions in golden fruit. It is a period of rejoicing, of congratulation, of feverish desire for more unsubdued wilds to conquer. As Uncle Sam stands upon the threshold of the new century, gazing with speculative eye upon the isles across the western sea where another inferior race awaits his pleasure,

243

he pauses in the work of conquest to jot down in his great diary this agent's memorandum of the inferior race at home:

" During the past fiscal year I have visited each and every reserve, even to those situated in the remotest districts. At many reservations I found the poor Indians eking out a miserable existence, in a half-civilized condition, with never enough food and clothing to sustain them properly, and as a makeshift making pilgrimages to the Sierra Madre Mountains, in Mexico, to gather the pine nuts for food during the pinching days of winter; yet I will give them the credit, even under greatly adverse circumstances, many of them were trying hard to raise something from their small patches of dry ground."

Vale, Mission Indian! Struggle as you may to gather sustenance from your gravel patch; fill your belly with the acorn, the pine nut, and the mesquite bean, if you will; but the day is coming when the white man will need your gravel patch; when his genius will devise some use in his own economic system for the acorn, the pine nut, and the mesquite bean.

Vale, Mission Indian!

And fifty years from now, when the more venturesome among the Noble Free — free from every restraint not imposed by themselves upon themselves, free to pursue happiness to the limit of their own desires — shall have exercised their God-given rights for a half-century in the new island country of the Pacific, will the United States Government be recording the woes of little native bands in the mountains and canyons of the Philippines, " eking out a miserable existence in a half-civilized condition " ?

Possibly the mountain fastnesses of the archipelago do not grow acorns, pine nuts, and mesquite beans? Perish the thought! Nature cannot have been so cruelly improvident of future necessities for the unhappy people who have hopelessly sung for their own country —

> " Land where my fathers died,
>
> · · · · ·
>
> From every mountain-side,
>   Let Freedom ring ! "

DIVIDING THE SPOILS

IN the pioneer days of fifty, forty, and even thirty years ago, when settlement on the frontier meant something of hardship and privation, the homestead law, with its provision for a small fixed charge upon every homesteader without regard to differences in land values, served to reward the hardy pioneer for pushing out beyond his neighbors by bestowing upon him the first choice of soil and location. Not only was he rewarded in direct proportion to his hardihood by this system of "first come, first served," but the Government and the country at large gained as well, in the development of new territory.

In preparation for this great westward movement, the Indians of the plains and mountains were from time to time gathered upon reservations; those east of the Rocky Mountains were located, in the main, along the Missouri River on the north, and within the Indian Territory on the south. The advancing civilization of the white man came up with these reservations, established itself alongside them, and pushed on westward to the natural limit.

Ouary, Ute Chief, Colorado
(1874)

been equally bound in its manner of dividing the spoils.

What has always been the result?

Instead of the Government beckoning to civilization to people its wilderness, we find it announcing the day and hour set for the opening of its public land. The fixed price per acre is but a fraction of its value; Uncle Sam gives the Faithful the full benefit of his sharp bargains with the Indians. The military parades across the tract to keep it clear of "sooners" — an expressive term applied to boomers who enter the promised land sooner than they ought; on the day of the opening, soldiers with loaded rifles are posted in front of the hungry horde, with orders to shoot if the line is overstepped — and they have shot, too, with telling effect; adventurers take the place of *bonâ fide* settlers, and alluring Chance supercedes reasonable expectation of reward for labor.

The evils and abuses attending the "rush" system reached their culmination at the opening of the Cherokee Strip, on the northern border of the Indian Territory, in September, 1893. The reader cannot better comprehend this method of dividing the spoils than by attending, in retrospect, this most grotesque event.

A hundred thousand men stand in line on land in Kansas and Oklahoma worth from ten dollars to twenty-five dollars an acre, gazing upon land to be offered at the crack of a gun for one dollar and a half and two dollars and a half an acre. That is the measure of the Government's bargain with the Indians. Some have been there for weeks, some for months — why so long, nobody knows; neither do they. The shrewd ones have been waiting no more than a day or two; they and their horses are fresh for the rush. Twelve o'clock is the hour set for the opening, and on the last morning of the long wait a deep, suppressed excitement possesses the motley crowd, growing more intense as the forenoon wears away.

They begin to form for the great race. The cowboys in front with their hardy prairie horses, ready to swear to each other's "time" before the land office officials — for after the race each must prove the time of his arrival if several enter claims for the same tract. Men with race-horses, too, confidently take their places beside the scrubby cowponies; but they will not ride their thoroughbreds next time — racers do not understand about badger-holes and gopher-mounds; very few cow-ponies ended that race with broken legs. Then there are horses in harness; sulkies, buckboards, spring buggies, and even lumbering lumber wagons, — prairie schooners, tops and all, loaded with stoves, and chairs, and babies, and chickens, with now and then a pig thrown in; sure signs, these, of the nomadic, renting farmer, the all-wise, know-nothing, soldier of misfortune, the typical western renter.

Dividing the Spoils

You find him everywhere, this sage of the corner grocery; in the West he is the nomadic renter. In the fall, to begin with, there is the renter and his family, fresh from their latest failure. He bargains for a broken-down team and mortgages it back to the owner for the full price, — the owner is pleased to have his team fed through the winter. He borrows a cow for her " keep " and increase, then rents a farm " on shares "; the owner furnishes the seed, and rewards himself liberally in the lease for doing so. The winter passes somehow, with odd jobs; by spring he had delivered a course of lectures at the country store on How to Run the Government, and the store-keeper holds a mortgage on the crops " to be " for supplies advanced. Now he half plants his crops, and tends them — hurriedly; for he is needed at the store to explain grave defects in the national currency system. Harvest time comes, and he " buys " machinery; another chattel mortgage. But the lightning of misfortune never misses him; if too wet, his crops wash out; if too dry, they burn out; for they were never really *in*. And he lays it all to the currency.

After the harvest comes the accounting. The land owner helps himself first, then the store-keeper; the machinery goes back to the factory, and the owner of the team claims his own. Last of all, the source of his milk supply ambles out through the gate in the wake of her unfeeling master.

The Indian Dispossessed

So, once more in the fall, there is the renter, and his family — plus one. The annual cycle is rarely left incomplete.

Months ago the renter heard of the great Cherokee Strip opening, and started forthwith for the promised land. He has been camping out all the way down from Io*way*, or Illi*noiay;* he has been camping here for weeks. But for the first time in his life his cock-sureness wobbles a little; there is something in the determined looks, in the be-pistoled figures of the line in front that dispels his dream of a home for the asking. Deluded renter, you are only one of fifty thousand! This is to be a race for the swift, not for the settler.

The great, lumbering wagon cannot make the run — he gets *that* through the armor of his self-conceit. So he proceeds to " on-hitch " his least " winded " plough-horse, and gets astride; and as this Don Quixote outfit shuffles to the front, the children squall, and the chickens squawk, while his long-suffering, much better half tearfully prays that this once in their dreary lives good fortune may smile upon them.

Over there is a man standing beside a rough stone set in a little mound of earth; that stone is a section corner. He is talking in a low tone with two or three friends; the quarter section of land marked by that stone is worth four thousand dollars, and it will cost some lucky man two hundred and forty.

Dividing the Spoils

As he thinks of it his breath comes hard, and his eye has a dangerous light. He turns to his friends. Will they bear witness that at the crack of the gun he was the *first* to claim this tract? Will they stand by him?

His friends gaze down the line of thousands and turn apprehensively away; they have seen the same dangerous light in too many eyes that morning.

Each man has a little flag to thrust into the ground as soon as he thinks he has reached a square half-mile of land without a claimant. But suppose there is another flag, and another claimant? Well, each man has a little gun, and if he can convince his unwelcome neighbor by argument that he is the better shot, there need be no bloodshed.

It lacks fifteen minutes of twelve o'clock. The tension of the supreme moment brings silence to the trembling line, save only low mutterings over the final adjustment for places. Men who have never seen a hundred dollars at one time in their lives now see thousands in their grasp if only they can place themselves among the winners; and there are five men to every prize. Out one hundred yards in front, and twice as far apart, stand soldiers with loaded rifles. Some, already drunk with the anticipated excitement, care more for the game than for the stakes to be won or lost, but to many a man in that line who has staked his last dollar on the one chance to win more than he can ever earn, those

The Indian Dispossessed

last minutes are a long, hot agony of suspense.
Suddenly a revolver is accidentally discharged; a
middle-aged man, in the frenzy of the moment, mistakes it for the starting gun, and with a bound his
horse shoots over the line.

" Hold on there! Come back!" yells the crowd
in wild discord, and the man imagines the crazy
horde racing at his heels.

" Halt!" commands the soldier in front, bringing
his rifle to position; but the man hears nothing, sees
nothing, thinks of nothing except the prize ahead.
The soldier drops to his knee, and aims; there
is no report above the din of the excited mass at
the line — only a puff of smoke; the old man
topples from his horse — dead, with a bullet in his
brain.

Twelve o'clock. The report of the signal gun is
echoed down the miles of line from every soldier's
rifle, and with a dull roar that makes the earth
tremble the racers are off! Horsemen, buggies,
buck-boards, wagons, as far either way as one can
see — and prairie schooners, too, lumbering and
pitching in the rear. Away over the rolling prairie
they speed, disappearing finally on the distant hills
like a lot of scared jackrabbits, now well strung
out. Suddenly a trained race-horse goes down —
he has learned his first lesson in badger holes. A
bullet from his master's gun ends the animal's suffering, and with him goes his master's last chance.

Dividing the Spoils

It is sixty-six miles across the strip, but another line is racing up from the south. Half-way, if they run so far, the unlucky ones in the two lines must meet, and turn back.

On they go, with now the fleet horsemen well out of sight ahead, and the prairie schooners as well out of sight behind. It is hot, — a hundred in the shade, and no shade; and dry, — no rain has fallen for weeks, and not a green thing is to be seen; no water anywhere, and a strong head wind.

There is smoke ahead — a prairie fire! The cow-boys in advance, impelled by a cheerful desire to impede those following, have fired the dry prairie. The grass is short, and a prairie fire runs ahead of itself in spots; it is easy to get through the breaks in the fire-line — if the grass is short. But word comes along the line that the fire has caught a schooner in the tall grass of a ravine, — and there is one less family to people the new country.

The boomers are continually dropping off to plant their little flags — some one will get this land, and why not they? Here a man finds himself in a wide stretch with no one near; he " strikes," then leisurely searches for the corner-stone. A school section. " Damn! " And he has no second chance, for the line has swept past him.

Four sections out of every thirty-six reserved for school and county funds, but with nothing to distinguish them; so one out of nine of the *successful* racers must draw blanks in Uncle Sam's great game of chance, in spite of their success.

A young fellow has run thirteen miles in the front rank of the line, and locates a beautiful tract, but he comes upon a man calmly smoking, while his horse grazes peacefully near, with not a hair turned. "Sooner!" angrily charges the young man; then he suddenly looks down the barrel of the sooner's gun. It is a wicked little black hole; the young man sees the point of the argument, and gallops on.

Down in that ravine are a few trees — there are no trees, except in ravines. There is something unusual about one of these trees. Go nearer, and a man hangs from one of the limbs. A slip of paper is pinned to the coat:

"Too Soon"

Nothing more; a brief but comprehensive epitaph.

A determined boomer plants his flag on a tract of fine bottom land — the prettiest quarter section in sight, he notes exultingly. A young tenderfoot from "back East" unwittingly plants *his* flag on the same tract. He thinks he is first, and perhaps he is. He approaches the boomer to expostulate, and the boomer draws, but the tenderfoot is not familiar with that line of argument. A shot; and a pretty home in New York State will wait and wait for news of its adventurous son. The boomer turns from the shivering form to the little half-mile of land danc-

Dividing the Spoils

ing in the hot sun before his feverish eyes, and mutters, " Mine, *mine!* "

Which of these two is the more miserable victim of the Government's gambling scheme?

Evening comes, and with it the wind dies down. The dry air quickly cools. The great rush has left its members scattered over the prairie — far too many of them for the rewards it had to offer, but the interminable fights, disputes, and lawsuits over the spoils are for other days. A short communion with the pail of cold grub and the canteen of warm water; then to the blankets, under nature's canopy.

It is a glorious, still night out on the prairie. The heat, the dust, and the wild excitement seem like unpleasant incidents of long ago. The heavens in that clear, dry atmosphere are fairly ablaze with stars; one cannot gaze into their quiet depths and realize that within the past few hours one hundred thousand men have indulged the fiercest of human passions, and for higher stakes than they have ever before dreamed of. But relaxation comes after unnatural stress, and men begin to know how tired they are; so winners and losers alike roll up in their blankets to sleep. The delicious calm of the night is made weird by the far-off, long-drawn-out cries of the boomers, calling the numbers of their land: "My — number — is — section — township — range —. K-e-e-p — o-f-f!" Then, after each call, crack! goes a rifle, as added warning; now from one direction, perhaps plainly, and again from another, so far away that little more than the faint report comes out of the darkness.

With the rising of the sun comes the wind, and then the heat; higher wind, and more fierce heat. Everybody is astir. Some start back for Kansas — the exodus of the unlucky begins early. Others head for the land office, farther south, to file their claims, and many flock to the towns which have sprung up over night along the railroad. A mushroom town is a jolly thing to see — and then to get away from. All through the night freight-wagons and the railroad have been bringing merchandise and material to the town-site, and the stuff is piled everywhere. Already the lucky winners of town lots have put up tents, braced against the howling wind, and a few have begun work on their cheap frame buildings. It is a busy day in this dust-swept town for the noisy, unwashed multitude, and Sunday at that. Sunday, and from an improvised pulpit under the railroad water-tank, a preacher delivers the first sermon to a very small but not select audience, while a lively vaudeville show farther along gives the town its first suggestion of paint. But carpenters, merchants, teamsters, and boomers of every description are too busy with the first business of their town to give much attention to either.

A tented restaurant springs from the ground; only black coffee and biscuit, but the coffee is *hot* — what

Dividing the Spoils

a relief from cold grub and warm water! Business is rushing, and long arms are reaching over the crowd in front. Then some one announces, "Lady coming!"

A lady! Instantly, respectfully, the crowd makes a clear way to the counter, and here comes the lady — Heaven save the name!

A bedraggled, unwashed, sand-biting human creature like the rest of us, but a female withal; she may be the forlorn wife of some boomer, or she may be the remnant of a trim maiden schoolma'am from "back East." There is no telling which; twenty-four hours next to nature have obliterated all distinguishing marks. She shuffles up to the booth, gets her creamless coffee and butterless bun, and shuffles off again.

But there is chivalry for you, put to the severest test and not found wanting. Plenty of men in that crowd who will fight, and shoot if necessary, for a prize in Uncle Sam's great lottery, but a respectable woman is safer there than on many a city street.

But human nature, and good nature, cannot long stand under these strenuous conditions, and now the exodus is on in earnest. Even the winners are ill-prepared to live in a treeless, waterless country from which nothing can be gathered for a year. Back to civilization the boomers wearily march, on horseback, on foot, in wagons,—and the prairie schooners again, with their stoves, and chairs, and babies, and chickens, — but what a changed lot from the expectant, excited boomers of a few days ago! Worn out, dirty, disgusted; supplies gone, money gone, hope gone, and cursing their luck. Many corner stores, if the orators succeed in getting " back home," are going to hear caustic lectures on the mistakes of the Government.

So this motley crowd of disappointed boomers works its passage back to Io*way*, and Illi*noiay*, and to all the other ways which had known them before the great fever to get something for nothing took possession of their senses. Some — good sports, good losers — laugh at their own folly, and thank Heaven for returning sanity. Others stare into the face of ruin — they had burned their bridges behind them, and are stranded, perhaps with families, in a strange land. And the families? The strangers' corner in many a Kansas cemetery can show little mounds — and sometimes larger ones — made in September, 1893.

And what was it all about? Did they want land to cultivate, land on which to establish homes?

Not one in ten, for not one in ten of the winners made homes of their winnings more than long enough to get their patents and sell out.

It was the value in this land *above the Government price* — the value which the Indian had given up in his bargain with the Great Father — that

Dividing the Spoils

brought these adventurers from all parts of the country. It was the wild chance to come in for a share of their Government's spoils that aroused them to a gambling pitch.

Deluded fools! They furnished a boom for the new country, and left millions of their good dollars in the land of the Vociferous Few who had engineered the whole scheme. Easy victims!

A grotesque method, this, for settling the public domain. But the opening of the Cherokee Strip was an object-lesson in governmental rectitude compared with the latest developed scheme for dividing the spoils in the Indian country. Not until the year 1904 did the Vociferous Few demonstrate to what length a half-dozen men can safely go, with the aid of a willing Congress, in the gentle art of buncoing the Indian and hoodwinking the public.

UNCLE SAM, TRUSTEE.

"By the President of the United States of America: A PROCLAMA-
TION: Whereas, by an agreement between the Sioux tribe of Indians
on the Rosebud reservation, in the State of South Dakota, on the one
part, and James McLaughlin, a United States Indian inspector, on the
other part, amended and ratified by act of Congress approved April 23,
1904 (Public No. 148), the said Indian tribe ceded, conveyed, transferred, relinquished, and surrendered, forever and absolutely, without
any reservation whatsoever, expressed or implied, unto the United
States of America all their claim, title, and interest of every kind
and character in and to the unallotted lands embraced in the follow-
ing-described tract of country now in the State of South Dakota, to
wit. . . ."

THE public is thus informed of the manner
in which a portion of the Rosebud Indian
reservation was added to the public domain. The proclamation then proceeds to explain
in detail the method of opening these lands to
public entry under the general provisions of the
homestead law.

It is proposed to show —

That the above statement intentionally conceals the
truth, and misleads the public into the belief that
the act of Congress taking these Indian lands was
in accordance with an agreement with the Indians.

That no agreement with the Indians existed bearing the faintest resemblance to the provisions of this
act.

SPOTTED TAIL AND SQUAW
(1877)

Uncle Sam, Trustee

That by this act Congress took over the Indian lands on terms of its own, which were never submitted to the Indians for their approval.

That Congress alleged an agreement with the Indians as a basis for the act when no such agreement existed, for the studied purpose of covering up the confiscation of nearly one million dollars of Indian land value.

To prove the truth of these accusations one need not go beyond the range of facts easily accessible, but their serious nature compels a discussion of this one event in the affairs of the Rosebud Indians, to the exclusion of a more general history of the tribe.

As a premise it will be sufficient to say that the Rosebud Sioux, numbering about five thousand, occupy a large reservation in the southeast corner of the original great Sioux reservation. For a considerable distance its eastern boundary is — or was, until the act of 1904 moved it westward — the Missouri River; Nebraska lies on the south, the Pine Ridge reservation joins it on the west, and to the northward is the great cattle range country of South Dakota.

It was to the Rosebud country that the great Sioux Chief Spotted Tail led his dissatisfied people, when, in 1878, he evacuated the Ponca homes so kindly placed at his disposal by the Government. For the accommodation of Spotted Tail the Rosebud agency was established, and a large portion of these Indians to-day are the old followers of Spotted Tail, or their descendants.

By far the greater part of the Rosebud reserve lies within the area of insufficient rainfall, and is good only for grazing. The increase in altitude is rapid as one goes westward from the Missouri River, up the great slope that leads to the Black Hills, and then to the Rocky Mountains beyond. But in the vicinity of the Missouri River are large sections of exceedingly fertile agricultural lands; in fact, the only strictly agricultural lands on the whole reserve lie at its eastern end. Naturally, then, the eastern end became of especial interest to the land speculators.

In respect to cessions of land the Sioux nation has sustained a relation to the Government differing greatly from that of other Indian tribes, by virtue of an iron-clad article in their fundamental treaty of 1868, known as the treaty of Fort Laramie:

"Article XII. No treaty for the cession of any portion or part of the reservation herein described which may be held in common shall be of any validity or force as against the said Indians unless executed and signed by at least three-fourths of all the adult male Indians occupying and interested in the same. . . ."

There is a directness of intent in this article not often found in Indian treaties. No treaties are made with Indians which are not for cessions of land; consequently, instead of representing the consent of a few favored chiefs, every treaty or agreement since 1868 with any of the numerous Sioux tribes has been compelled to exhibit the signatures of three-fourths of the adult males concerned. If one wonders how an Indian treaty happened to contain a provision so sweeping, so certain in its meaning, and wholly without the usual convenient loophole, " at the discretion of the President," or some other authority vested in the party of the first part, — a trick that has let the force out of nearly every Indian treaty, — he should remember that in 1868 the Sioux nation could muster as many warriors as the whole United States army was able to send against them; the settlements of the great Northwest, the Union Pacific railroad, — then building, — and at times even the army itself, were at the mercy of such powerful chiefs as Spotted Tail, and Red Cloud, made desperate by what they regarded as the invasion of their country, and the extinction of their game. The treaty of Fort Laramie was no one-party affair; but even under the stern necessity of securing protection for the frontier and the cessation of hostilities, it is to be doubted whether this covenant would have found a place in the treaty without some undermining provision attached, had its lasting import been fully realized.

Coming at once to the events directly concerned in this discussion, in the summer of 1901 United States Indian Inspector James McLaughlin negotiated an agreement with the Rosebud Indians for the purchase of 416,000 acres at the eastern end of their reservation. This tract included the entire frontage on the Missouri River, and practically all of the agricultural land on the reservation. Nearly one-half of the tract, however, consisted of strictly grazing land, worth but little more for stock-raising purposes than the western portion of the reserve left to the Indians, except that it was nearer to the river and to transportation facilities.

The price was fixed at two dollars and a half per acre, or one million and forty thousand dollars; nearly half of the sum was to be paid to the Indians, in money and live stock, upon ratification of the agreement, the remainder to follow in four annual cash installments.

The agreement was signed according to the treaty of 1868 by 1031 Indians, that number, as the agent certifies, " being twelve more than three-fourths of the male adult Indians of the Rosebud reservation."

Although, according to a subsequent report of no less an authority than the Honorable Commissioner himself, " when the agreement of September 14, 1901, was being concluded, the Indians argued with great persistency that their lands were worth more than two dollars and a half per acre, and they were almost unanimous in declaring that they were well worth five dollars per acre," it is not the intention to question here the methods used to obtain the agreement, but to accept it as *bonâ fide*. The farming land was, of course, worth several times two dollars and a half per acre, but the grazing land would, in 1901, have scarcely sold for one dollar and a half.

This agreement was to be binding upon the Indians " when accepted and ratified by the Congress of the United States." A bill embodying its provisions was presented at the next session of Congress, but it was *not* passed; in the vernacular of Washington the bill was " killed " somewhere among the committees. The agreement, consequently, was not accepted nor ratified. The explanation current at that time for the failure of the scheme was that it was then inexpedient to ask Congress for the large appropriation required to pay for the land.

Beginning with 1901 a most remarkable wave of land speculation swept over the West like a tremendous thunder-shower, leaving a rain of gold in its path. The storm seemed to centre first in South Dakota, and like most storms in the Northwest it moved northward. After delighting the hearts and filling the pocket-books of the North Dakotans, it finally spent itself in the Canadian Northwest. Land values in South Dakota were doubled, then trebled; in many instances they were quadrupled within two years. At no time, curiously enough, even in the height of the buying, was there any considerable immigration of permanent settlers; the buyers were mainly wealthy farmers and country bankers from Iowa and adjacent States, augmented by a considerable force of chronic speculators from everywhere. Not in a dozen years had so much land been sold as in the two years of this speculative boom. It was a natural reaction from the long period of land depression which followed the disastrous western mortgage business of the eighties, and as a net result of the general shaking-up, South Dakota found herself in 1903 with normal, steady land values averaging throughout the State somewhat more than double those which prevailed prior to the welcome raid of the speculator.

This kaleidoscopic change in the land situation served to intensify, as may be imagined, the sincere sorrow of the South Dakota delegation in Congress over the loss of a good bargain with the Indians. But it is in the philosophy of the professional land-grabber that " while there 's an Indian there 's hope "; pressure was again brought to bear upon the Department of the Interior, and in the summer of 1903 Inspector McLaughlin was again on the Rosebud reservation, endeavoring to obtain a renewal of the old agreement, modified, however, in one important particular, so as to avoid the necessity of asking Congress for any considerable appropriation. Instead of the Government buying the entire tract outright at two dollars and a half per acre, as previously proposed, the Indians were asked to let the Government, as *trustee,* open the lands for white settlement at the *same* flat price of two dollars and a half, pay the Indians the money only as collected from the settlers, and guarantee neither the sale of *all* of the tract, nor the payments.

Here was a tract of land representing extremes of value; rich agricultural land, worth five dollars, ten, and some even twenty-five dollars per acre, on the one hand; on the other, grazing land hardly salable at two dollars. The Indians failed to see why they should let the *choice* of their land go at the *average* price for the *whole,* and be left with the poorest on their hands. The reasonableness of their position is apparent; a merchant having a stock of cloths, part silks, the rest cottons, might fairly name a flat price per yard for the entire stock of both silks and cottons; but were he, in a fit of mental aberration, to open his store to the retail trade at that same flat price per yard, first come first served, the public would end the day with rare bargains in silks, and the merchant — with a stock of cottons.

Moreover, the Indians refused to renew the former agreement to sell the entire tract at the two dollars and a half rate; a syndicate of capitalists had recently offered the Commissioner of Indian Affairs five dollars per acre for the same tract, and to this figure they persistently clung.

Thus the scheme failed. The Indians had the temerity to demand from the Government the same price offered by a speculating syndicate, and the device intended to capture the good land for a song, without taking the poor, failed to entrap the Indians.

Viewed from the professional boomer's standpoint, there is nothing to be gained by opening lands to public settlement at somewhere near its value; it is not the *land*, but the *value above its selling price,* that is depended upon to bring a rush of prize-seekers into a new country. The greater the value to be given away, the more deluded fools with money will struggle with each other for the few prizes, and the greater the resulting boom.

The South Dakota statesmen were sad. Inspired by the good old saw, " if at first you don't succeed," they had tried again — and failed again. But there is in the philosophy of the sanguine land-grabber another bit of cheer, equally inspiring — " if again you don't succeed, try Congress."

In Washington, " far from the madding Indians," the schemers then gathered together and drafted a bill after their own liking for taking over the Indian lands. Here is their beneficent proposition :

The Indians were to " cede, surrender, grant, and convey to the United States all their claim, right, title, and interest " to the 416,000 acres, excepting the allotments to individual Indians.

Next, " The United States stipulates and agrees to pay for sections sixteen and thirty-six, or an equivalent of two sections in each township, two dollars and fifty cents per acre," and to deliver it to the State of South Dakota for school purposes. These sections — two in every thirty-six — were all that the Government was to pay for.

All the remaining land — some 382,000 acres — " shall be opened to settlement and entry by proclamation of the President," the price to be, " upon all land entered or filed upon within three months after the same shall be opened for settlement and entry, *four dollars per acre*,[1] to be paid as follows: one dollar per acre when entry is made; seventy-five cents per acre within *two* years after entry;" and seventy-five cents each year thereafter until paid for. This delivered to the land-grabbers the entire body of agricultural land, worth four, ten, fifteen, and in some instances twenty-five dollars, at the bargain-store price of four dollars, and on terms so easy as to suit the most vociferous.

Then, as to the lands below the four-dollar mark — comprising about one-half of the entire tract — " Upon all land entered or filed upon after the expiration of three months and within six months after the same shall be opened for settlement and entry, three dollars per acre," with the same dollar paid down, and *fifty* cents annually after two years. Of course, very little land not taken at four dollars would go for three dollars: this provision was a

[1] In the original draft of the bill the maximum price was three dollars; these quotations are from the act as passed by Congress.

mere pretentious showing of a sliding scale of prices, designed to cover the *main attack* on the left-over lands.

This final steal was a clever piece of work. The value of these grazing lands was not much below two dollars and a half per acre, even under the handicap of the homestead law, which required a nominal residence of at least fourteen months upon the land; another wave of speculation, or a couple of good cattle years, would double, perhaps treble, their value — and such a turn in the market might come at any time.

So, in anticipation of the happy day, the plotters decreed that all land left over from the first two sales was to remain open to homestead entry at two dollars and a half per acre for a period of *three and one-half years* more; and finally, any land " remaining undisposed of at the expiration of four years from the taking effect of this act, shall be sold and disposed of for cash, under rules and regulations to be prescribed by the Secretary of the Interior."

Thus, if the grazing lands should advance to five dollars, the Indians would get two dollars and a half; if prices should remain stationary, or decline, the lands were to be sold for whatever they would bring. The land-grabbers were to take the gain in values, and the Indians the loss.

And the last words of this precious act carefully

explain that Uncle Sam does not " guarantee to find purchasers for said lands, or any portion thereof, it being the intention of this act that the United States shall act as *trustee* for said Indians to dispose of said lands and to expend and pay over the proceeds received from the sale thereof only as received, as herein provided."

Three separate peculations were developed in this scheme:

First, the Big Steal — the confiscation of every dollar of Indian value above the four-dollar-per-acre mark.

Second, the Long Steal — the four-year open game of " heads I win, tails you lose," for the grazing lands.

Third, the Little Steal — the taking by the Government of some twenty-three thousand acres at two dollars and a half — exactly half the price offered by the syndicate.

Thus the Rosebud bill was drafted. To give it any measure of reputable standing, the endorsement of three-fourths of the male Indians was absolutely essential; but their endorsement was out of the question.

One other way was open to the conspirators, — that was to take advantage of a recent decision of the Supreme Court, abrogate the time-honored Sioux treaty, and take the land without the Indian consent.

On January 5, 1903, the Supreme Court of the

The Indian Dispossessed

United States, in deciding the Lone Wolf case, declared that " The power exists [in Congress] to abrogate the provisions of an Indian treaty." This sweeping declaration was attended by many suggestions of limitation, of caution, and of the grave responsibility laid upon Congress to exercise this trust with due regard for the national honor:

" Presumably such power will be exercised only when circumstances arise which will not only justify the Government in disregarding the stipulations of the treaty, but may demand, in the interest of the Government and the Indians themselves, that it should do so." And again, " In a contingency such power might be availed of from considerations of governmental policy, particularly if consistent with perfect good faith toward the Indians."

Still again the decision bears upon Congress its moral responsibility:

" We must presume that Congress acted in perfect good faith in the dealings with the Indians, . . . and that the legislative branch of the Government exercised its best judgment in the premises."

In this decision the Supreme Court virtually pronounced the death sentence upon the Indian's treaty rights, with the supplication — " And may Congress have mercy on his soul!" as though it feared the worst.

Indian treaties since the beginning have never been deserving of the name of " treaties "; nearly every stipulation in the Indians' favor has been provisional, ambiguous, or directly subject to the discretion of the Government. "Articles of Guardianship" would have been a better name for the fairer ones, and "Sharp Bargains" for the majority. Though professing to be treaties, at no time have they had the standing of treaties made with the most insignificant of outside nations — and in the very nature of things such recognition was impossible. Yet for one hundred years the United States hypocritically bargained with the aborigines under the guise of treating with competent nations. The name "treaty" was abandoned in 1871, although the business has since been continued under the name of "agreements."

The appalling feature of this radical decision of the Supreme Court lies, not in proclaiming the hollowness of these treaty farces, but in the naming of the Indian's guardian — Congress, the amiable Pontius Pilate of the Indian race, always ready to yield to the clamor of the Faithful! It is impossible to estimate the disasters that may come to the Indian as a result of this decision. The Indians' friends have welcomed with one accord the breaking up of the reservation system, the allotment of lands in severalty, and the curtailment of rations — but with these steps in advance comes the necessity for the sale of the surplus Indian lands. At this critical time, when the proper establishment of the Indian in his new relation as an individual demands that his small remaining patrimony be most conscientiously realized upon, he is deprived of all voice in his own affairs and the disposal of his land goes into the general stock-in-trade of that great political trading-post, Congress.

But over this doubtful course through the congressional clearing-house the South Dakota statesmen hesitated to send the Rosebud bill. There was nothing in it to "justify the Government in disregarding the stipulations of the treaty"; the interest of the Indians was *not* considered; it was wholly "*in*consistent with perfect good faith toward the Indians."

Nothing but an unadorned display of its arbitrary power to "abrogate the provisions of an Indian treaty" would enable Congress to pass this bill. It might as well be labelled, "An act to confiscate all value in the Rosebud lands above four dollars per acre, and deliver it to the Faithful." That would have been an honest title, and the power exists in Congress to pass just that kind of a bill.

The land schemers discarded the open course as too dangerous. Nothing remained but to railroad the bill through under color of the Fort Laramie treaty. In the absence of an agreement with the Indians, it became necessary to *allege* an agreement, so the discarded agreement of 1901 was resurrected and attached to the bill.

It was a plain agreement to sell the entire tract

276

Two Strikes, — Brulé Sioux

(1878)

outright to the Government at two dollars and a half per acre; it bore not even a family resemblance to the provisions of the proposed bill; it had been once presented and refused in Congress, and later repudiated by the Indians; land values had more than doubled in the two years which had elapsed; but what of it?

"An agreement with the Indians" — that so disarmed general suspicion, both in and outside of Congress, that the Indians' friends protested almost in vain when the bill appeared in January, 1904. Reuben Quick Bear, President of the Rosebud Indian Council, appealed to the Indian Rights Association:

"If ever we needed help we need it now, and badly. . . . A real estate man recently went over it and told a friend of mine that he would gladly give $10 an acre for the whole tract, and could raise the money in three weeks. Over a year ago a syndicate offered the Commissioner $5 per acre for the whole tract, and land around here has since doubled in value. We only ask $5 per acre. . . .

"Ask that three men be appointed to value the land — one to be appointed by the Commissioner of Indian Affairs, one by the Indians, and these two to select a third, as was done when the Omaha reservation was valued years ago. If this proposal is entertained the South Dakota delegation will at once consent to $5 per acre, as they well know that any half-way fair valuation would be far more than that. . . ."

But the South Dakota delegation did not propose to have daylight let into their scheme by three impartial appraisers.

Newspaper articles appeared, scoring the bill in language picturesque. A periodical of the highest authority on current affairs came out with a broadside against the bill, denounced both the scheme itself and its "agreement" disguise, and strongly urged a competitive sale of the lands under homestead restrictions as the only sane, honorable method of realizing for the Indians the full value of their surplus lands. But land everywhere is offered at competitive sale; boomers do not rush in to spend money for land offered at its value.

Congress was not without official information and advice during its deliberations. The Honorable Commissioner of Indian Affairs, in reporting the bill to Congress, had this to say:

"When the agreement of September 14, 1901, was being concluded, the Indians argued with great persistency that their lands were worth more than $2.50 per acre, and they were almost unanimous in declaring that they were well worth $5 per acre. . . . In fact one offer was made by parties to take all the lands covered by the cession at the rate of $5 per acre. . . .

"The Indians cannot see . . . why they should

not procure such price for the lands as settlers are willing to pay for them. The Indians in their talks have shown themselves to be not unreasonable in their demands, but simply persisted in demanding what they believed to be just and proper. . . ."

Whatever may have been the shortcomings of Indian Commissioners in years past, the Indian office during the last few years has been administered by sincere friends of the Indian. There is nothing in the Indian situation more gratifying than this, at a time when the last of the Indian's patrimony is absolutely at the disposal of Congress.

But the efforts of the Indian Rights Association and the plain statement of the Commissioner served only to raise the maximum price, originally three dollars, to four dollars per acre. Nothing but a thoroughly aroused public opinion can move Congress, and public opinion could not be aroused in the face of "an agreement with the Indians."

Then, with the declaration, " That the said agreement be, and the same hereby is, accepted, ratified, and confirmed as *herein amended and modified,* as follows: " — the Rosebud bill became a law in April, 1904, as though an agreement between two parties, changed out of all resemblance to its original self by one of the parties without the consent of the other, were entitled to the name " agreement "!

Thus ends the first act in the Rosebud land scandal. The second has to do with the division of the spoils.

The Indian Dispossessed

The Rosebud bill provides, " That the lands ceded to the United States under said *agreement* . . . shall be opened to settlement and entry by proclamation of the President, which proclamation shall prescribe the manner in which these lands may be settled upon," etc., but at the prices and terms set down in the act.

Never before had such acute conditions been confronted at a distribution of public land. The Rosebud tract bordered upon well-settled, prosperous farming country; adjacent railroads and cities furnished the necessary elements for a most prodigious boom; immense value above the four-dollar price was to be given away; and, with it all, the West was land-crazy. The usual " rush at the crack of a gun " was out of the question. The stakes were too high. Frenzied boomers would tear each other to pieces.

A very different scheme was adopted for the distribution of the Rosebud lands. Instead of the fierce rush at a given signal, the choice of lands was to be determined by a lottery drawing. This system was first devised in 1901 for the opening of a somewhat remote tract of Indian land in the Indian Territory, but it lent itself well to the purposes of the Rosebud opening. The President's proclamation fully sets forth the plan:

" Each applicant who shows himself duly qualified will be registered and given a nontransferable certificate to that effect, which will entitle him to go upon and examine the lands to be opened hereunder. . . .

"The order in which, during the first sixty days following the opening, the registered applicants will be permitted to make homestead entry of the lands opened hereunder, will be determined by a drawing. . . . Preparatory to this drawing the registration officers will, at the time of registering each applicant who shows himself duly qualified, make out a card, which must be signed by the applicant, and giving such a description of the applicant as will enable the local land officers to thereafter identify him. This card will be subsequently sealed in a separate envelope which will bear no other distinguishing label or mark than such as may be necessary to show that it is to go into the drawing. These envelopes will be carefully preserved and remain sealed until opened in the course of the drawing herein provided. When the registration is completed, all of these sealed envelopes will be brought together at the place of drawing and turned over to the committee in charge of the drawing, who, in such manner as in their judgment will be attended with entire fairness and equality of opportunity, shall proceed to draw out and open the separate envelopes and to give to each inclosed card a number in the order in which the envelope containing the same is drawn."

Then the lucky thousand or so first out of the box were to choose their prizes in the order of their numbers.

And the rest? Merely blanks.

The distribution of public lands under the time-honored homestead law was thus resolved into a game of chance, from which every element of reward for personal achievement had been eliminated, — a simon pure lottery, with the price of admission a trip to the land office. As a lottery, its absolute fairness was vouched for by the Government; but the Government is on record as unequivocally opposed to lotteries of all kinds. The spectacle of Uncle Sam treading upon his own toes is, of course, paradoxical, but these parallel quotations are significant in view of the wide circulation of the President's proclamation through the mails:

FROM THE PRESIDENT'S PROCLAMATION:

"Each applicant will be notified of his number, and of the day upon which he must make his entry, by a postal card mailed to him at the address given by him at the time of registration."

FROM THE U. S. POSTAL LAWS:

"No letter, *postal card*, or *circular* concerning any lottery, so-called gift concert, or other similar enterprise *offering prizes dependent upon lot or chance*, and no list of the drawings at any lottery or similar scheme . . . shall be carried in the mail."

Uncle Sam, Trustee

" The result of each day's drawing will also be given to the press to be published as a matter of news."

" Nor shall any *newspaper*, circular, pamphlet, or publication of any kind . . . containing any list of prizes awarded at the drawings of any such lottery or gift enterprise, whether said list is of any part or of all of the drawing, be carried in the mail."

Possibly there is some technical evasion of liability under the law; but who will say that the *spirit* of the law was not violated? The United States postal laws, and the several State laws directed against games of chance, do not presume fraud; they aim to protect the people from the demoralization that comes from tempting offers of opportunity to get something at less than its value, — something for nothing.

The effect on the people of this " circular . . . offering prizes dependent upon lot or chance " can be readily guessed. Relieved of apprehension as to life and limb, guaranteed " fairness and equality of opportunity " in a simple game of chance where the turn of a card meant hundreds, or thousands — or nothing — the gambling spirit was aroused as the Louisiana lottery never aroused it. By hundreds from the Eastern States, by thousands from the Central West, men flocked into South Dakota to " play the game " with Uncle Sam. Nearly three weeks

283

were consumed in registering the multitude of applicants. Hamlets of a few hundred became temporary cities of ten thousand. Gambling breeds gambling, and professional gamblers from all parts of the country catered to the absorbing passion of the day. "Never in the palmy days of Deadwood was gambling more rife," writes one correspondent; "just about every game ever invented, with the single exception of policy, can be found in one or more of the public resorts." The carnival of crookedness led to open defiance of the authorities, but the better element among the boomers, after a pitched battle with the crooks, finally succeeded in checking the lawlessness. The casualties of both sides covering the whole summer campaign in the Rosebud country were between twenty and forty, including both killed and wounded. Twice during the excitement formal demand was made on the Governor for State troops, but the Governor seems to have wisely concluded to let the motley crowd "fight it out."

After the registration came the drawing.

There were twenty-four hundred homesteads in the entire Rosebud tract. Of these, a thousand were prizes well above the four-dollar mark.

For a chance to draw these one thousand prizes, 106,296 individuals had registered their applications. The game stood one hundred to one against the players.

Uncle Sam, Trustee

Remote as was the chance of drawing a lucky number, never was a gambling game conducted more fairly and squarely than this one. Every move in the grand final event was religiously referred to Mistress Chance. First, boxes containing one thousand each of the 106,296 envelopes were numbered, and the order in which they should be emptied into the one big drawing-box was determined by lot. On the theory of "first in, last out," this preliminary event narrowed the probable winners down to the last few thousand cards deposited in the big receptacle. Then, from among eight boys named by the drawing committee, four were chosen by lot to draw the numbers in turn from the box. Again the boys' names went into the hat, and a third drawing determined the order in which the four lads were to draw the envelopes.

Finally, Boy Number One, all ready to draw Prize Number One, was photographed beside the precious box while the expectant throng held its breath.

Prize number one — the best one hundred and sixty acres on the Rosebud — perhaps next to a townsite — or a vantage point on the Missouri — wherever the winner might choose to locate his little fortune — fell to a clerk in the United States Treasury Department at Washington. And the first one hundred winners fared nearly as well. About twelve hundred entries were made at the four-dollar-per-acre rate.

The Indian Dispossessed

But the losers? One hundred and five thousand of them. This tells of only one:

"One old man stood near the edge of the platform, looking with anxious interest at the drawing. Clerk John McPhaul, who was in charge of the Bonesteel office, whose heart is as kind as a woman's, saw the old man and beckoned him to come to the stage and offered him a chair. But the old man was too interested to take a chair. All during the three days' drawing he hovered just over the chairs of the clerks who were taking the names of the lucky drawers. On the second day he was at his post when the drawing commenced, his old, weather-beaten face tense with anxiety. The third day found him still at his post, anxious, but still hopeful. That he was expecting to draw a claim became noised around, and every one was hopeful that the old man would be lucky. When the last number was drawn and his name had not appeared the old man looked about in a dazed sort of way and shuffled off the platform. His shoulders were bent and it was easy to see that he had suffered a deep disappointment. That old man was probably a type of thousands who were scattered throughout the country."

And the rake-off? One hundred thousand pilgrimages to the promised land, at an average of twenty dollars each — *two million dollars* of expense money left with the South Dakotans; this is *more*

Uncle Sam, Trustee

than twice the sum that will be paid to the Indians for the lands taken; more visitors, and more visitors' money, than South Dakota had seen in ten years. Did it pay? Of course it paid. What would a sane, competitive sale at fair value have been, compared to this?

Who furnished the prizes? The Rosebud Indians, — the erstwhile followers of the powerful Spotted Tail. In 1877 we saw the Poncas driven by Congress into worse than Siberian exile that it might reward Spotted Tail for his valiant services in securing peace with the Black Hills Sioux. Now we see the dwindling remnant of Spotted Tail's people robbed by Congress that it may pay its political debt to the stalwart South Dakota delegation.

And the Steal? The entries made at both the four-dollar and the three-dollar rates will yield, if all entrymen pay in full, about $850,000; but after the first excitement, many will never make the second payment. What the Indians will eventually get for the remaining lands is problematical, — the four-year game of " heads I win, tails you lose " is now on for the grazing land. Taken as a whole, a guaranteed return of one million dollars for the tract would have been a better sale for the Indians; they could have sold for two million dollars. The steal? Approximately one million dollars.

CONCLUSION

HERE is the spectacle: a government founded on the principle of equal rights to *all men*, securing to its own citizens equality of opportunity and fair play, while it persistently denies both to the Indian. The people earnestly desire justice for the Indian — of this there is no question. Congress is made up of the people's representatives, and Congress, ignoring the general sentiment, has from 1789 to 1904 persistently, steadily borne down upon the Indian in the interest of the few in the Indian country.

Curiously enough, each individual writer of Indian history sees the short cut to reform through an appeal to the American people.

Bishop Whipple of Minnesota, who gave the best part of his life to the Indian cause, declared, after recounting the acts of broken faith which led up to the great Sioux massacre of 1863, "I submit to every man the question whether the time has not come for a nation to hear the cry of wrong, if not for the sake of the heathen, for the sake of the memory of our friends whose bones are bleaching on our prairies." This bookful of wrongs, and volumes more, have been perpetrated since.

LITTLE CROW, LEADER OF SIOUX IN THE MINNESOTA MASSACRE
(1863)

Conclusion

More than twenty years ago Helen Hunt Jackson closed the preface of her "Century of Dishonor" thus: "It is a shame which the American nation ought not to lie under, for the American people, as a people, are not unjust. If there be one thing which they believe in more than any other, and mean that every man on this continent shall have, it is fair play. And as soon as they fairly understand how cruelly it has been denied to the Indian, they will rise up and demand it for him." And the century of dishonor has lengthened by another quarter.

Col. Richard I. Dodge, after thirty-three years on the plains as Indian fighter, displays in his "A Living Issue" this same confiding hope: "It is too much to expect any one of these [politicians] to risk the loss of votes and thus jeopardize his future career for a miserable savage. Politicians will do nothing unless forced to it by the great, brave, honest, human heart of the American people. To that I appeal! To the press; to the pulpit; to every voter in the land; to every lover of mankind. For the honor of our common country; for the sake of suffering humanity; force your representatives to meet this issue."

This was written more than twenty years ago. What is the matter with "the great, brave, honest, human heart of the American people"? Nothing. But a "government *of* the people" has not much to boast of if, when so constituted, it fails to be a

"government *by* the people." This persistent miscarriage of good intentions leads to the inquiry
whether the Government really does represent the
people.

It is the ideal of statesmanship that statesmen determine questions of national policy on broad lines
of national expediency, without undue regard for the
more narrow desires of their respective constituents;
but it is enough to expect of the average representative that on all questions his views will be more
or less colored by the interests of those to whom he
looks for support. Assuming that each member of
Congress is indebted for his office directly to the
people, and not to other combined interests (but
what an assumption!), there is no menace to the
public welfare in this narrower statesmanship; the
resultant of their legislative efforts will be along
the line of greatest good to the greatest number.

But the main business of Congress — or, rather,
of congressmen — is not the determination of national issues. The final measure of a congressman's
political usefulness is his ability to secure a fair share
of governmental favors for his district, and for his
political supporters. Harbor and river improvements,
fortifications, dry docks, arsenals, federal buildings,
irrigation plants, and ten thousand and one desirable
federal offices, — all these are within the gift of
Congress, and every congressman has a right to indulge the hope that, with reasonable endeavor on

Conclusion

his part, these favors will be dealt out to him in fair proportion to his political representation. In general, each section has its own particular desires, and is scarcely interested in the ambitions of its neighbors except as they affect its own ambitions. The seaboard town urging the betterment of its harbor is indifferent to the construction of jetties in the Missouri, while a dry dock appeals to the western member charged with securing an irrigation appropriation merely as having an unpleasantly suggestive name.

It is no more than natural that from these conditions there should have developed in Congress an elaborate system for the exchange of support in the business of securing these local favors; in view of the expectations of his constituents, it is not only natural, but necessary, that a congressman, even a conscientious congressman, study the distribution of his influence as much with reference to the returns it will bring in exchange as to the merits of the schemes to which he lends it. Even in this business — and it is strictly business, not statesmanship — there need be no menace to the national honor; to gain strategic advantage for one good cause by skilfully advancing other good causes, is good business.

But the descent from the ideals of statesmanship to the realm of hand-to-hand business is a descent from the forum of public discussion to intrigue and private agreement. In this lies the danger. A not too close scrutiny of the projects to which he gives his approval brings to the congressman a greater measure of support; in turn, if his supporters are equally accommodating, his own demands for governmental favors may safely assume questionable proportions. Every tendency within the system is reactively downward; constituencies, knowing little of methods, are quick to recognize success; and it is the natural tendency that only " successful " men are returned to Congress. With the strengthening of this class comes increased opportunity under the peculiar methods of the trading system.

Now, among these numerous favors at the disposal of Congress place the American Indian.

" But," you say, " harbors, and dry docks, and federal patronage are material things, reasonably to be trafficked in; with the Indian and his affairs you introduce the human element, — you place the welfare of human beings on a level with mere chattels in the political market."

That is just where the Indian has been for one hundred and twenty-five years, — a valuable asset in the general stock, to be manipulated and exchanged with as little regard for the human interests involved as though his lands and all things material to his welfare were no more than harbors and dry docks. A western district covets the best portion of an Indian reserve; the way to the Indian land lies through Congress, and the business is placed with the dis-

Conclusion

trict's representatives. The support of delegations from other Indian reserve districts comes as a matter of course, — they may in turn be called upon to perform a like service for their constituencies. Together, they are an influence in Congress which can determine the success or failure of a dozen other projects — and they are intent upon advancing only this one. What, then, is easier than to convince the ardent seekers after river improvements, and public buildings, that their scheme is one of sheer philanthropy for the Indian? A few "gentlemen's agreements," judiciously placed, and the business is done.

Why should the whole villainy of it be charged to the western member? Could a scheme such as the Rosebud bill, exposed as it was to *every member* of the Senate and House of Representatives, have passed the *honest* scrutiny of members who could have had no possible selfish interest in the bill? In the midst of the general barter, is it in human nature that the western member should not bring his influence into the market-place, and offer it for his one desire?

Under this system the Indian, although ostensibly giving up his substance to his western neighbor, has indirectly been an unwilling subscriber to the thousand and one benefits distributed by Congress to the people the country over. There is in this a reason for the almost inexplicable persistence of the one dishonor that has run the whole length of the na-

The Indian Dispossessed

tional life. Under the very system of government which is supposed to secure to all men an active participation in its benefits, the Indian's vital interests — establishment upon *good* land, with protection and equality of opportunity during his long endeavor to adopt the new civilization — are hopelessly entangled with the merely sordid, commercial side of national legislation. In all the conglomerate mass that makes up the nation, he is the only human factor without representation by vote; he has no political asset with which to gain consideration for himself from a government which apportions its consideration according to representation.

Thirty years ago a Commissioner of Indian Affairs delivered himself of a fervent opinion which should become classic. The miserable story of the California Indians had dragged itself through twenty-five years; every measure of relief had been blocked in Congress by the interested few, — the Vociferous Few in the Indian country. "This class of Indians," concludes the Commissioner, "seems forcibly to illustrate the truth that no man has a place or a fair chance to exist under the Government of the United States who has not a part in it." A more illuminating commentary on the Indian's unhappy status in the land of the Free can hardly be written in one sentence. The Indian's story does not argue that the Indian should have been at any time given the protection of the franchise; but it *does* argue that in

294

RED CLOUD, THE OLD-TIME WARRIOR
(Totally blind, 1903)

Conclusion

a loose-jointed republic where national legislation is at the beck and call of every little coterie of irresponsible voters, the Indian has been subjected to more devilish variations of human caprice than if he were at the mercy of an openly oppressive, but more consistent and centralized style of government. There is no despotism more whimsically cruel than that of men unused to power, who suddenly find themselves in absolute control of a people whose one vital interest — an advantageous foothold on *good land* — is in continual conflict with their own chief desire, — the possession of that same good land.

It is a boast of the American people that no flagrant wrong can long persist against an opposing public opinion; that the remedy is with the people, and the people will apply it. Now, although grounded as this Indian iniquity has always been on the very principles of " government by the people " which place the remedy in the people's hands, why has public opinion, so often aroused, failed to dislodge it?

Suppose the representative of a particularly virtuous district in New England were to take a determined stand against some unjust Indian legislation, not only threatening its success, but disturbing, possibly, other projects before Congress dependent upon a general exchange of support. And suppose the overwhelming majority in Congress which recognizes the expediency of the trading system were to punish this obstreperous member by sending him back to his constituents without the benefits and patronage to which he is fairly entitled. His constituents may vigorously applaud his action in the Indian matter, but will they recognize it as balancing his failure to secure the new post-office building which they had a right to expect? If they do, will the memory of the righteous act endure until the next election day against the continual, daily want of the material thing? And even if the voters' sentiment carries them to this unusual length, will the political managers, the office seekers, who really sent him to Congress to *get something*, and to whom he is primarily accountable, permit his name to again appear on the ballot?

The answer to these questions is safely a negative one. Behold, then, the wide distribution of responsibility for this melancholy Indian business! Considering its intimate connection with the material, commercial favors which come to all the people through their Congress, is its persistence so inexplicable as it might seem? And did ever an iniquity more subtly fasten itself upon the very shoulders of a people intent on promoting virtue!

No wonder it persists. And under the same conditions any other evil which appeals to the selfish interest of the few can persist, *because it indirectly promotes the selfish interests of the many*. That which can be done in Congress by an irresponsible community can be done by *any other irresponsible*

Conclusion

combination with the requisite showing of political influence. What better can a people expect of legislators whom it virtually holds to the business of legislation by private agreement, than that they will also make private agreements on their own individual accounts? Congressmen have only to maintain a reasonable showing of returns to their constituents from the system of legislative barter, to effectually kill the kind of public sentiment that lacks the inspiration of some selfish interest. In effect, the people are without representation in Congress as regards their moral convictions.

The Indian iniquity, and these other evils, will persist as long as the irresponsible community stands equally with other communities in the ease with which it can secure legislative enactments, restrained only by such vague moral considerations as may in Congress survive the exigencies of the trading system. They will persist until the people are willing to give up some of their freedom in order that a few may not be too free; until there is toleration for a central authority which shall restrain the irresponsible community, as the communities themselves restrain the irresponsible individual.

There is no quick remedy in an appeal to the people. The remedy must go deep into grounded notions of what constitutes freedom and what really is government by the people; then it may reach that institution of perverted functions, Congress.

The Indian Dispossessed

The prime requisite for the advancement of the public good is to instil in the public mind a deep, persistent distrust of the National Congress. Only by stirring to the depths can there come lasting good.

HELEN JACKSON'S WORK.

A KEY TO "RAMONA."

A CENTURY OF DISHONOR.

A Sketch of the United States Government's Dealings with some of the Indian Tribes.

A New Edition. 12mo. pp. 514. Cloth. $1.50.

Mrs. Jackson devoted a whole year of her life to writing and compiling materials for "A Century of Dishonor," and while thus engaged she mentally resolved to follow it with a story which should have for its *motif* the cause of the Indian. After completing her "Report on the Condition and Needs of the Mission Indians of California" (see Appendix, p. 458) she set herself down to this task, and "Ramona" is the result. This was in New York in the winter of 1883-84, and while thus engaged she wrote her publisher that she seemed to have the whole story at her fingers' ends, and nothing but physical impossibility prevented her from finishing it at a sitting. Alluding to it again on her death-bed, she wrote : " I did not write Ramona;' it was written through me. My life-blood went into it, — all I had thought, felt, and suffered for five years on the Indian question."

The report made by Mrs. Jackson and Mr. Kinney is grave, concise, and deeply interesting. It is added to the Appendix of this new edition of her book. In this California journey Mrs. Jackson found the materials for "Ramona," the Indian novel, which was the last important work of her life, and in which nearly all the incidents are taken from life. In the report of the Mission Indians will be found the story of the Temecula removal, and the tragedy of Alessandro's death, as they appear in "Ramona." — *Boston Daily Advertiser.*

Mrs. Jackson's Letter of Gratitude to the President.

The following letter from Mrs. Jackson to the President was written by her four days before her death, Aug. 12, 1885 : —

To GROVER CLEVELAND, *President of the United States :*

Dear Sir, — From my death-bed I send you a message of heartfelt thanks for what you have already done for the Indians. I ask you to read my "Century of Dishonor." I am dying happier for the belief I have that it is your hand that is destined to strike the first steady blow toward lifting this burden of infamy from our country, and righting the wrongs of the Indian race.

With respect and gratitude,

HELEN JACKSON.

LITTLE, BROWN, & CO., Publishers

254 Washington Street, Boston, Mass.